ONLY YOU SATISFY

A Memoir of How Finding Love in Italy Helped Me Bloom

Kio Lashei

Library of Congress Cataloging-in-Publication Data
Kio Lashei
Only You Satisfy: A Memoir of How Finding Love in Italy
Helped Me Bloom

Edited by Jerra Latrice and Callie Walker
Cover design by Francisca Mandiola

Library of Congress Control Number: 2020918965

ISBN: 978-1-7358954-0-6

Printed in the United States of America

Note: The events, the experiences, and the places mentioned in this book are real and actually happened and have been set down to the best of the author's ability, although the author has taken the liberty to change names and details to protect the privacy of the individuals.

This is for the one and only true love of my life.

CONTENTS

INTRODUCTION

The Donut Man. Have you heard of him? If you grew up as a Christian in the '90s, you probably remember his songs. My mom would play his music on cassette tapes most of the time whenever we were in the car. At night, she read either Psalm 91 or Psalm 103 to me and my brother. Although I knew both of those chapters by heart from the King James Version, I didn't have a deep relationship with God.

I also didn't have a close relationship with my dad, so I carried an emptiness inside and a looming sadness over me for many years. Somehow, God was enough to fill that up. On the other hand, because my dad was not around, I searched for fulfillment and validation from guys. I had also unfortunately been aroused at the age of five, and shortly thereafter, I saw images of people doing things that still plague my mind to this day. Because my innocence was stolen, and my father was not active in my life, it created a recipe for thirst (from the attention of other men) to rain down full force. The intensity of it all just had not hit me at that point.

When I went off to college, I purposely made it my mission to fill up my schedule with anything that kept me occupied. I joined a club called InterVarsity, which was the Christian club on campus. We would have "small group" and "large group." At the time, I'd never heard of those words. In small group, we would just have Bible study with other college students, and then on Thursdays, we would all gather to have worship, then listen to a message. No one ever told me that going to college meant that I would grow closer to God. In fact, while most people were smoking, drinking, doing drugs, pulling all-nighters, and having sex, I was in my dorm room reading my Bible, hanging with my roommates, or doing some fun activity with InterVarsity.

This was when I learned what it meant to have a relationship with God. It meant that I could just spend time in His presence. I didn't necessarily *need* to ask for anything. I could just praise Him, pray, read my Bible, and receive from Him. I could just be. I was the happiest I had ever been in my entire life. The presence of the Lord was overflowing in me. I also had a job that allowed me to do homework if I had downtime, and I would use much of that time to spend with God.

My third year in college resulted in a move off campus and a moment with God. I sat in my kitchen where I had been working on my homework, and for some reason, I started thinking about a guy whom I'd had a crush on for about nine years. I had seen him when I was twelve years old and was so captivated by how attractive he was that I wanted him to be mine. He never paid any worthwhile attention to me no matter how loud I laughed or how well

I dressed, and we had never said more than, "Hi, how are you?" to each other. This crush was built on a superficial foundation, yet it was extremely difficult for me to give up on the hope that he would one day be my husband. As I was thinking about my crush, I also started thinking about my dad and if I should continue pursuing a relationship with him. He rarely called me, and when he did, I always said something that made him so angry that he'd ignore me for months and sometimes years until he felt like talking to me again. That day in the kitchen, I felt God beckoning me to start working on healing my "man problem," which was a result of my daddy wound.

Surprisingly, while I was in college, boys weren't necessarily my priority. I only made out with one guy who kissed so horribly that I pushed him away, ran back to my dorm room, and wrote a poem about his kissing. After that experience, any guy that showed me attention quickly got the cold shoulder from me. The reason I didn't pay much attention to guys around me was because I still had hope that I would end up with the guy I had a longtime crush on. Well, God wanted me to completely release any delusion I had about being with that guy.

In my time with the Lord, I would give Him bits and pieces of my hurt and my feelings of unworthiness and wanting to be loved, but never all of it. It seemed like every time I would start to dig into that wound, I was reminded of how unwanted I was by my own father, and by the boys that I desired, that I would just end up crying and feeling worse about myself. The shame from my past was too much to bear. Not wanting to feel that pain, and wanting my time spent with God to be happy, I stopped digging into that wound and made up my mind that I would work on it "later."

Working on it later also meant that I spent less time with God as a result. I stopped going to InterVarsity, figuring that I was fine on my own. The Lord had filled me up so much in the previous years that I felt I didn't really need Him anymore. I would read my Bible here and there, but I wouldn't seek God as intentionally because I knew that He would want me to go into that mental place that I didn't want to go.

This was also around the time that I started seriously thinking about studying abroad. At this point, it was between Canada and Italy since I didn't have too many options because of my major. This was also when I noticed a difference in my mood and my happiness. I was never diagnosed with depression, but I classified myself as slowly sinking into a depression because I just simply wasn't myself anymore. Life started to feel like a drag. I was crying all the time, and my thirst for a man was rising up even stronger. I thought I was crying more because I had made a decision to study abroad. That decision required a lot of emotional maturity. Whatever it was I told myself, I never connected it to spending less time with God.

When my fourth year came around, I knew it was time to go abroad because everything just felt right, and I had finally saved up enough money. After deciding on Florence, Italy, I was paired with a mentor who had studied in Florence the previous year. We would meet every Wednesday, and he would just sit and talk to me about his experience while answering any questions I had. Then, one day I found out that I was accepted into the program, and everything became so surreal. I would be going abroad the way I had wanted to.

I wanted my time in Florence to be a romantic getaway with God where I would reconnect with Him. I wanted His love to overflow inside of me, like natural spring water you drink after hiking up the tallest mountain on the hottest day. I wanted His love to constantly spring up inside of me so that I didn't have to look elsewhere for it.

This book is a retelling of the ten months I spent living in Florence, Italy, with all of the ups and downs, the highest highs, and lowest lows, along with the lessons I learned about life, love, and God.

Chapter One

TURBULENCE

HAVING A DIRECT flight from Los Angeles to Florence is much easier than stopping over in a random city somewhere. Without a layover, you board your flight, you eat, you read, you watch movies, you sleep, and you wake up a thousand miles away from home at your destination. Easy. I wasn't made to wait at airports for nine hours. Layovers were made for backpackers or people who regularly traveled to foreign countries by themselves.

"Mommmm," I moaned, closing my laptop. I dragged myself out of bed and I opened the door to my room.

"Mom," I called down the hallway.

"Yes princess," she said in her soft voice.

I poked my head around the door and frowned.

"They changed my flight to the one I didn't want."

Her head jerked back and she sat up in bed. "Oh, wow."

I plopped myself onto the edge of the bed.

"I don't want to wait," I said, sticking my bottom lip out.

"Well, you should call them."

"Oh." I perked up. "I guess I should, huh?"

"I'm sure they can change your flight. There is always something that can be done."

How does my mom know literally everything?

"Okay, I'll call them now," I said.

After an hour of back and forth with the agency, I was put on a much earlier flight. I was now set to leave two hours after I landed in Rome. *Thank God.*

I played with my dog, took a walk around my neighborhood, and checked my items again, before loading my two suitcases into the car and heading to the airport with my mom. When we arrived at LAX, my mom came with me to check my bags in. At the check-in station, I was handed only one of my boarding passes and was told by the woman helping me to get my other boarding pass once I landed in Rome. *Weird, but, okay.*

There were a lot of tears, hugs, and kisses as I said good-bye to my mom. It took all of my strength to pull away. I looked back at my mom as I rode the escalator up to the second floor. After going through the security checkpoint, I sat at the gate to wait for my flight. While I was waiting, I met two girls from my study abroad program. Their names were Britney and Mia. We sat in the gate for about two hours talking and sharing how we felt about the entire upcoming experience. I had Wi-Fi in the airport, so I was able to text my mom before we boarded the plane. The twelve-hour plane ride was so pleasant that I felt as if I was riding in first class, even though I clearly wasn't. I sat next to a woman who was spending two weeks in Rome to take a cooking class, and we spoke throughout the flight whenever I wasn't asleep or reading.

Once we landed in Rome, Britney, Mia, and I stuck together and followed the crowd to security. I was stopped from being able to go through security because I didn't have my second boarding pass. So, I was told by one of the personnel to go downstairs to the Alitalia desk. I don't remember saying a word to the clerk at the desk because I was too nervous to speak. She seemed to know what to do because she said, "Go to Terminal One," as she handed me a piece of paper.

"Umm, okay, thank you," I managed to mumble while holding the paper.

Once I went through security, I checked the flight status board to find my gate. I saw that my flight was boarding at gate C5 at 5:30 p.m. A feeling of uneasiness came over me. *Why did she tell me to go to Terminal One if my flight was boarding somewhere else*? I shrugged and walked away. I passed the time by messaging one of my friends, who was kind enough to update my mom on my status since, for some reason, I was unable to contact my mom. Two hours flew by, and I said farewell to Britney and Mia and got in line to board my flight. A woman (about two people in front of me) handed a piece of paper over to the lady checking the passes. She looked at the paper, shook her head, gave the paper back to the woman, and pointed upstairs. She signaled for the next person without missing a beat as the woman, clutching the piece of paper, scurried away, looking frazzled and confused. My heart sank for her.

I was signaled to come forward and the lady took my pass and examined it.

"You cannot board with this," she said in perfect English. My mouth went dry, and my heart sank even deeper than it had earlier.

"What do you mean?" I took the paper back and looked at it.

"Go upstairs," she said, waving me to the side and signaling for the next person. Instead of arguing with her, I jumped out of the line and followed the woman who had been denied before me. We ended up at an Alitalia station and I walked over to one of the clerks. I did my best to calm my nerves before saying, "I wasn't able to board my flight. Can you help me?" She sighed, snatched the paper from my hand, and scribbled some words on it.

"Go see if they will let you board now," she said, looking right through me.

Back downstairs, I got in line and then handed the woman the paper.

She sighed and mumbled to herself.

I told her that I went upstairs, and all they did was write on the paper. She went to her computer and typed, then called someone on the phone and spoke in rapid Italian. When she finished, she turned to me and said, "You need to go upstairs."

Tears fell down my face as I walked back to the same Alitalia desk that I had been at five minutes before. This time, I went to go to a different woman, and I told her what my dilemma was. After typing on her keyboard, she told me that the flight I was trying to board was now ready for takeoff. I asked if I could be put on the flight that I was trying to avoid: the one that left at 9:30 that evening. She typed on her keyboard again.

"I cannot change the flight," she said.

"I need to get to Florence," I said, holding back my tears.

"Go over there," she said.

I saw her finger pointing to an airline station with the word "Milan" written on the wooden desk. I went up to a clerk and told her what my issue was. The woman told me that she could do nothing for me since they only dealt with flights that flew to and from Milan. I went back over to the Alitalia station and was once again told to "Go over there." Back at the Milan desk, I spoke to a different woman, and even though she told me that she could only deal with flights related to Milan, she took my pass and looked at it.

"This is not a boarding pass," she said.

"Umm… what? Can I see?" I asked, furrowing my eyebrows.

"Yes," she said and handed the paper back to me. "What you have is only a confirmation that you checked in. I'm sorry, I cannot help you to change your flight. You will need to purchase another ticket."

"I'm so confused," I said, sniffling and wiping my wet eyes. "They…they gave me the paper downstairs. I didn't know it wasn't a boarding pass."

"I am sorry," she said. She pursed her lips and shrugged.

"Can you… there's a flight that leaves at nine thirty. Can you get me on that flight?" I asked, frowning and looking down at the desk.

She took the paper from me and walked over to a computer. I heard her typing on the keyboard. I took this time to wipe my face and take deep breaths.

"I am sorry. I cannot do anything to your ticket. It seems there is a block on your ticket," she said.

I sighed as she wrote on the ticket.

"There is the number to the agency. You can call them."

All I had on me was a low-battery iTouch, which I was using to frantically message my aunt, asking her to call the travel agency for me. I felt like collapsing on the ground and curling up into a ball. I took a deep breath and looked to my left. There was a lady sitting alone. I walked up to her and asked if I could use her phone to make a call. She gave me a weak smile and shook her head. I sat down to take a breather and prayed. With my eyes closed, I thought back to a passage from the book called *How Faith Works* written by Dr. Frederick K. C. Price. This was the book I was reading on the plane. In the book, he explains a concept called "faith" that all Christians, those who have accepted Jesus as their Lord and Savior, possess. Faith is something that you do! I remember reading in the book that faith speaks and perseveres. Even though I felt in my deepest feelings that I was not going to leave Rome and make it to my destination that night, I ignored how I felt and whispered, "I am getting on the flight that leaves tonight at nine thirty."

I looked up and saw a pay phone, which I decided I would use to call the travel agency. As I tried to put coins into the slot, my jacket, pieces of paper, my fake boarding pass, and other things fell to the ground. I was trying not to look flustered, but it wasn't working. I reached down to pick up the paper that had the travel agency's number on it. I felt a tap on my shoulder. I looked up and saw the woman from the Milan desk.

"It's okay. Come with me," she said.

I exhaled. I picked up all of my things, retrieved my coins from the phone, and followed her over to the Alitalia station that I had been at earlier. She took me over to a man sitting at the desk and said, "He will help you out."

With a huge smile and the urge to hug her I said, "Grazie mille!" (Thank you so much!)

"You're welcome," she said and walked away.

The man gave me a standby boarding pass and I went over to the standby station where I was told by the clerk to come back at 8:55 p.m.

"Oh, okay. Thank you," I said.

Please let there be a pass for me.

Britney and Mia were shocked to see me again. I told them everything that happened and we talked until 8:15 p.m. when I decided that it was time to go back upstairs. As I waited, the standby desk started getting a bunch of traffic, so I got up from my seat and stood in a place to make sure that I would be seen. At 8:40 p.m., I was able to get the clerk's attention and tell him that I had been there earlier, waiting to be on the flight to Florence. He smiled and said, "A few more minutes."

I sat back down.

"I am getting on the flight that leaves tonight at nine thirty. I am getting on the flight that leaves tonight at nine thirty," I whispered to myself as I bounced in my seat.

My heart started pounding and I felt myself losing hope.

A voice came from in front of me. "Florence."

My mouth fell open and I jumped up, skipped over to the desk, and saw a pass waiting for me! I was so relieved! I jogged back to my gate and boarded my flight. Once I landed in Florence with Britney and Mia, we retrieved our bags and got into a taxi. When we arrived at the hotel at about 10:30

p.m., all I wanted to do was sleep since 9:00 the next morning was the start of my first full day in Florence, Italy.

...

I woke to the sound of loud engines roaring and horns honking outside my window. I was breathing in shallow inhales and exhales, barely able to suck in enough air to fill my lungs. The room was dark, but I could see the silhouette of one of my roommates outlined in the sheets. My other roommate was in the bed next to her. The air was fresh and cold. I let out a muffled sneeze as my nostrils came alive. I closed my eyes and saw fuzzy black-and-white dots dancing. I opened them and I looked around. Nothing looked familiar to me.

Who are those girls in my room? Where am I?

"Brrrrinnnnggg. Brrrrinnnnggg."

I looked over at the tan-colored object sitting on the table. Sheets rustled in one of the beds. I reached over to pick up the receiver.

"Hello?"

"Pronto. Questo é un wake-up call per Lei. Grazie," said the voice. (Hello. This is your wake-up call. Thanks.)

The line went dead. I stared straight ahead and set the phone back down. Next to the phone was my iTouch. I opened it, pressed the Home button, and saw the number 7:46 on the screen. I had about an hour to get ready, so I got up and dragged myself to the bathroom. The light was fluorescent and so bright that it reminded me of a hospital. My reflection was that of a bruised and battered, sleep-deprived person. Staring at myself, I saw the dark under-eye circles and crust

near my mouth. Once out of the shower, my roommates were
now up and moving around.

"Good morning. My name is Kayla."

"Hi. Nice to meet you. I'm Kio," I said, waving at her.

"What time did you guys get in last night?" Kayla asked.

"At around ten thirty," Mia said.

"Yeah, we were the last ones to arrive," I said, getting
flashbacks of being thrown around in a taxi and arriving at
this unfamiliar hotel.

"It's good that you guys made it," Kayla said.

"I can't believe we're here. Did you get a chance to look
around yesterday?" asked Mia.

"I found a small *tabacchi*, or whatever, down the street,"
Kayla said in her soft, melodic voice.

"Great! I *need* some coffee. I'm so tired. What time are
we supposed to meet for breakfast?" asked Mia.

"At nine," I said.

What am I doing here? My eyes started filling up, and a
large lump forced itself out of nowhere into my throat. The
sound of my breath slowly escaping my nostrils calmed my
heartbeat down to a slow drum beat. The calm allowed me to
put my shoes on, leave the room, and close the door behind
me. Once in the cafeteria with everyone, I sat at a table with
some people whom I had met before coming to Florence:
seven of them to be exact.

"I'm Kio," I said with a forced smile to the only two
people I didn't know. Everyone at my table was holding their
mugs, delightfully sipping their Italian coffee and espressos.
Smiles, laughter, and jolly chatter filled the room. My peers
were effortlessly peeling and eating bananas, munching on

strawberries, and chewing their croissants with ease. Some were wearing glasses, others had cameras hanging from their necks. I forced the dry pastry into my mouth, quickly chewing and swallowing it before my nausea could fully kick in. My stomach grumbled so loudly the sound was similar to atomic bombs being dropped in the desert. The more I swallowed and sipped, the louder the bombs erupted. My legs wouldn't let me stop shaking them. I felt light-headed, and looking around for a familiar face that I had known for more than a month proved to be a futile task. New country, new surroundings, new foods, new smells. Why would there be anything familiar?

"Buongiorno, ragazzi!" A powerfully deep, yet calming voice rang out in the room. (Good morning, children!)

My heart jolted. I turned to see a white man standing in the center of the room. He had white hair covering most of his head and furry, thick, white eyebrows that sat above his blue eyes and square glasses. His fluffy, white chest hair failed to hide itself behind his deep-blue polo shirt. Next to him stood a shorter man who had dark hair with one swoop of a grey streak on the right side, circular glasses, and who wore the demeanor of an excited young boy on his first day of school. He was carrying a backpack pushed under his armpit and up against his side like a purse.

These men introduced themselves as Sean Groomis—our director—and Fabio—*What did he do?* They walked us through the order of business for that day, had us gather on the narrow sidewalk outside of the hotel, and handed us those walky-talky looking devices that all Chinese tourists use when they travel in groups. Not only did I clearly not look Italian with the color of my skin, but with this yellow strap dangling from my neck, the word "foreigner" didn't need to be written on my forehead.

Through the humidity and blazing sun, eighty college students followed two men over cobblestoned streets around the city. Men and women drove by with a zoom of their Vespas. The smell of leather and sewage filtered through the air. Women clad in long lime green skirts with brown pigtails hanging from either side of their heads begged for money.

"Ragazzi!" proclaimed Sean Groomis. (Children!)

We were now standing in the middle of a crowded square. To my left was a caramel-colored building; the facade looked like it was built with textured blocks. A replica of *David* in front of the building was the object of everyone's fascination. Littered on the streets next to us, behind us, and in front of us were pigeons: grey, tainted white, and dingy-brown pigeons.

"Ragazzi," he said again, "listen closely. Please be careful. There are pickpockets all over. And another thing, when you are using the ATM—also called *bancomat* in Italian, that's good to know—always cover your hand when typing in your pin. Actually, someone got ahold of my pin and took money out of my account. Even if you use your hand or a piece of paper, always cover your pin."

After Sean Groomis finished his lecture, we were taken to look at apartments. I was tired and wanted to go back to the hotel after looking at two apartments. As everyone else shuffled in and out of the other apartments, I stood outside waiting.

"You're not going to look at this one?" Fabio asked. The closer I stood to him, the shorter he seemed.

"No, I'm actually going to be living with a family friend," I said with a hint of pride in my voice.

"Maybe you should look just in case it doesn't work out," he said.

"Mmmm …" I was pretending to think. "It's okay."

It was around five in the evening when we finally made it back to our hotel. A day full of walking, walking, talking, eating, more walking, listening, learning, and seeing had my brain feeling like it had just run a marathon that it hadn't trained for. All I wanted to do was be alone, sulk on my bed, and gather my thoughts. Kayla and Mia must've had the same idea because we were all lying on our beds having small talk when the phone rang. Kayla held the phone to her ear and cocked her head to the side. She held the phone out.

"It's for you," she said to me.

I looked at Mia, shrugged, took the phone from Kayla, and asked, "Hello?"

"Yes. Please come to desk. Thank you," said a man's voice.

"What did they say?" Kayla asked. I put the receiver back down.

"I don't even know. I guess I have to go to the desk," I said.

I dragged myself from my bed and took the elevator downstairs. The man standing behind the desk handed me a folded piece of paper. I opened it to see the following words written:

I see you 16:30. Okay? Tomorrow.

Signed,

Dulce

"Grazie," I said. I held the letter in my hand the same way one would hold a delicate flower.

...

With another full day of orientation completed, I went back to the hotel where I met Dulce and her sixteen-year-old daughter, Sienna. I was in a daze as they took me around Florence to look at some dorm rooms and apartments. The only matter of interest to me was going to see her place.

"Come pensi, Kio?" I came back to reality after hearing my name.

"What do you think ... of this apart-te-ment?" Sienna asked.

"Oh, um ... it's okay. I want to see your place," I said.

"Vuole andare a casa noi," Sienna said to her mom.

"Okay. Andiamo," said Dulce.

We got a bus ticket from a magazine stand and took a twenty-minute bus ride to her place. The bus sped up hills and barreled over bumps, barely screeching to full stops to let people on and off, and we arrived at the bottom of a hill.

"È lontano dal centro," Dulce said, letting out a giggle.

I giggled too.

"What did she say?" I asked, looking at Sienna.

"We ... we ... um ... very long live from center."

"Oh," I agreed.

The further we got from the bus stop, the more difficult breathing became and the faster my heart pounded. There are times when I can have a schedule packed full of activities, feel tired, but keep going on. This was one of those times. Although I had completed a full day of orientation, which meant lectures, signing papers, and hearing more stories from Sean Groomis, I was determined to make it to the top of that hill, even if I had to crawl. I was determined to see my new home.

I was out of breath as we walked upstairs and finally made it inside. I followed Sienna through the darkness into the kitchen where her mom was opening windows. My mouth dropped open, and the only word I could think was "Wow." I was staring at a life-sized postcard. Jagged but perfectly formed mountains met fog and plump clouds that blanketed the tops of the mountains. Streaks of reds, purples, yellows, and blues were mixed into the sky as if someone was painting right before my eyes exactly what my heart desired to see.

"Bello!" I exclaimed, with a big smile on my face. (Beautiful!)

If the rest of the apartment was as nice as this view, then I'd be happy to live here indeed.

"Ah vero!" Dulce said.

I think she was agreeing with me, then she continued, "Okay, Kio. You come. I show," she paused to chuckle, "room."

"Oh! Great," I said.

The moment I had been waiting for had finally arrived. I took one last longing look out of the window and followed Dulce into a room. Sienna was sitting on the bed messing with her phone.

"Sienna, aiutami per favore. Basta così. Dammi il tuo telefono," demanded Dulce.

"No!" Sienna exclaimed, before rolling her eyes and fixing them back on her phone.

I stood there wondering what they were saying. Dulce was running around picking up shoes, organizing books on a desk, and picking up clothes. I felt like I had arrived too early for a party and the hostess was cleaning up before more guests arrived.

"My mom is annoying," Sienna said to me like she had been practicing that very phrase to one day say to a native English speaker. My eyes got wide, then I scrunched my eyebrows as I narrowed my gaze at her.

"Her English is not good," Sienna said.

"Oh," I said.

"I have a boyfriend." Sienna looked up at me.

"*You* have a *boyfriend*?" How shocked could I sound without sending signals to her mom through my tone? Dulce was still picking things up, unbothered. "How old are you?"

"Seidici… umm… sixteen. I have sixteen years," she said.

"How old is your boyfriend?" I asked.

"He… oh! Eighteen years." Sienna smiled.

"Eighteen!" The word flew out of my mouth. I again glanced over at Dulce.

"He has car. He can drive … we … us."

I held back the urge to scoff right in Sienna's face as her mom plopped a pile of clothes onto the bed.

"Sienna!" shrieked Dulce.

"Don't tell my mom," Sienna said, casting a serious glance in my direction. *This chick is crazy.*

"So, where's *my* room?" I asked.

"Dov'è la stanza per Kio?" Sienna asked.

"Oh, si! Mi dispiace. Qui con Sienna. Kio, tu stai con Sienna, e io dormo nell'altra stanza con mio figlio," Dulce said rapidly, too distracted with shaking Sienna's clothes and folding them.

I waited for Sienna to translate, even though I felt like I knew precisely what Dulce had said.

"We share room," Sienna confirmed.

I immediately broke out in a hot flash, my chest tightened, and I felt my eyebrows scrunch yet again. I wanted to sound diplomatic and unbothered, but I instead sounded whiny and impatient.

"Well, how much would I pay? For rent?" I folded my arms as I waited for a logical response.

"To stay?" asked Sienna.

"Yes," I said, the word coming out with more irritation than planned.

"Quanto costa per la stanza?" Sienna asked her mom.

"Seicento euro," Dulce said without an ounce of hesitation.

That can't be what I think she's saying. I mean, I haven't mastered numbers yet, but that can't be right.

"Six hundred euro a month." Sienna's voice got lost in my thoughts as I contemplated making a break for the door. Sienna was crazy, and now, so was Dulce. If anything, moving into her home was doing her a favor, and I couldn't fathom how €600 a month to share a room with a crazy, hormonal teenager was a fair deal.

"I thought I would have my own room." I hadn't planned to say that out loud.

"No. It is not possible." As the last word was falling out of Sienna's mouth, Dulce was shaking out a pair of her jeans. With one big swoosh, the jeans cracked in the air, spitting an object out of their pocket and onto the bed. Dulce quickly grabbed the object before Sienna could say anything.

"Sienna!" Dulce yelled.

Sitting in the palm of her hand was a pink lighter. If my Italian had been at a higher level at that time, I would've known everything Dulce screamed at her. One can only imagine. Sienna, with her smoking habit and creepy boyfriend, could keep that dusty, messy room for all I cared. Dulce could take her scamming somewhere else too. When the screaming fest was over, and I still felt like I wanted to jump out of the kitchen window and get lost in the picturesque mountains, I spoke to my mom, then told them I had to go.

Dulce and Sienna walked me to the bus stop, I hugged them, and got onto the bus. As the bus made the trek back to my hotel, I wondered where I would live. My thought didn't cause my blood pressure to rise or my heart to beat any quicker. A calm feeling came over me, as if I had just finished meditating. I didn't know *how* I would find a place to stay, but I *knew* that I would find a place to stay much closer to school.

I trust You, Jesus. I trust You.

...

The next day, I went to visit the perfect home—owned by an Italian family and surrounded by trees and mountains—with a girl from my school. I turned down the offer to live there. That house was also too far from school, and the amount I would have to pay to live there made my budget cringe.

What are you doing? You need a place to stay, and now you have nowhere to go, my mind screamed at me. So, I did what any mature twenty-one-year-old would do in such a dire situation—I spent my free time emailing family members, updating my blog, eating kebabs and margherita pizzas, and exploring the city.

One day, when I was out with some people from school, a girl I'd met once before walked up to me. Her square glasses covered her blue eyes, her blonde hair was slicked back into a ponytail, and her expression was neither happy nor angry, just there—emotionless.

"Hey, Kio. Are you still looking for a place to stay?" Lucy asked.

Looking? "Looking" was the loosest term she could've used. "Looking" implied that I was actively searching for a place to stay. On top of that, how did she know that I didn't have a place to stay? It's not like I was going around telling everyone of my imminent homelessness.

"Yeah… I am actually," I admitted.

"Eva and I need a third person for our apartment. You'll have to share a room with her. I'll have my own room. Is that okay?" she asked.

"Oh … y-yeah … sure. No problem." Even though I liked how she got right down to business, I was flustered by how she had showed up out of nowhere. "How much is rent? And where is the apartment?" I finally managed to get out.

"You'll only have to pay €300 plus utilities. It's near Santa Croce, close to school," she said.

"Fabulous, fantastic, sign me up!" I wanted to proclaim, even though all of this seemed way too good to be true.

"We'll just have to go to the housing office tomorrow to sign some papers."

I was a bit skeptical about accepting her offer, but I literally had nothing to lose and needed to let go of my pride.

"Okay, cool," I said.

The next thing I knew, Lucy, Eva, and I were putting our luggage into a taxi. We arrived at a beige and green apartment building and trekked up three flights of stairs as we dragged our suitcases behind us. With a click, the door numbered thirty-two swung open, and the feeling of being home welcomed me.

"This is you and Eva's room," Lucy said, catching her breath before disappearing down the hallway.

My room had two big windows on the south side. The east side of the room had a tall, wooden wardrobe. We both had wooden nightstands complete with lamps. Dark-pink-and-yellow checkered bedspreads added a splash of color to the whitewashed walls and hardwood floors. I walked over to my window, unlatched the lock, and pulled the window open with a loud swoosh. The swoosh broke the silence barrier, uncovering the sounds of activities happening below. I pushed the green shutters out in opposite directions so that I could observe what was going on. I heard horns honking and a bicycle's bell rattling as it skipped over the uneven pavement. A man and woman were walking alongside each other, holding hands. Cars lined the curbs. A man was across the street, one leg bent so that the sole of his shoe was pressed on the wall behind him. He was wearing black leather shoes, black slacks, and a white smock. A cloud of smoke covered his face.

Above him and directly across from my window was a balcony with what seemed to be a tarp behind it, covering a window. The balcony seemed big enough to hold a maximum of three people.

"Could you keep that open? It's so hot in here." Eva's cheerful voice broke me out of my trance.

"Yeah, sure," I said, pulling myself back into my room to see that Eva's bed was covered with clothes. My two suitcases were sitting in the middle of the room. I looked at them; said, "Excuse me," to Eva; and walked out of my room and down the hallway. At the end of the hallway, there was a wooden table with three wooden chairs. Behind the table was a bookshelf. On the far end of the room was a bright yellow, medium-sized couch and a cupboard, and to the left of that was Lucy's room. Off of the common room was a balcony with a washing machine. At the opening of the balcony were ropes strung to either end.

Next to the couch was a window. I opened it and leaned out to see a woman below tending to her roses. I looked to my right and saw bird droppings and grey-and-white feathers glued to a plastic covering that was draped over the balcony. A fat pigeon was perched on a window directly across from our balcony. We made eye contact and the pigeon seemed to arrogantly turn his face away from my field of vision. I huffed before going back inside and closing the window by twisting a knob to lock it.

Off of the living room was a kitchen equipped with a sink, two burners, an oven, and a refrigerator that overpowered the cramped space. As I stepped into the kitchen, the walls seemed to close in on me, forcing me into the bathroom. The layout of the bathroom ran horizontally so that the first item I came in contact with was the sink and mirror. To the left, the toilet was tucked into an alcove below a miniature window carved into the wall. To the right of the sink was a bidet and the shower. I snickered to myself about the odd layout of my humble, little abode. As odd as it was, it was my home.

My tiny, humble, and cozy apartment was only a fifteen-minute walk away from my school. My apartment would host Thanksgiving and Christmas parties, birthday parties, and hold the precious moments when I would spend time with God as I looked out at the garden below.

I can only attest to the fact that God worked behind the scenes to get me into that apartment because it was dropped into my lap. I was somehow showing God that I trusted Him. When things work out, they work out. You just have to trust God and know that He is working on your behalf. He had my back, and He has yours too.

Chapter Two

THE OUTSIDER LOOKING IN

I WAS STANDING IN the tiniest piazza in Florence—Piazza della Passera—with some of my schoolmates as we celebrated someone's birthday with gelato. Afterwards, I got lost with five friends as we tried to find Piazzale Michelangelo to catch a view of the city. We gave up on our quest and ended up hanging out at a bar along the Arno River as the sun descended. On most days, after class, I strolled around the city or found a place to eat pizza or a kebab with my friends. At night, when the lights from the city sparkled on the river, just walking and allowing the silence to speak to me was enough to keep me company.

Still, there were more days than not that I felt so utterly alone and that no one could understand what I was really feeling on the inside. Everything from learning Italian to going grocery shopping was so hard. There was a grocery store down the street from my apartment that I'd go to after class. The store was always crowded and always seemed to have the most impatient cashiers working whenever I went in.

On good days (I never knew when those were), I got a kind cashier who responded to my greeting of "Buongiorno." For a long time, I kept ending up in the line of the lady with the thin, brittle, burgundy, and barely shoulder-length hair. As edible items made their way down the one-foot conveyor belt, she quickly snatched, scanned, and tossed the fragile items to one side. I had to catch and bag my eggs, baguette, tomatoes, salami, and cheese while getting my euros ready to hand in for payment. Taking on these roles all at once always caused me to sweat as I struggled to multitask. While bagging the last of my items, my concentration was suddenly interrupted by a stern voice.

"Ventitré euro e novanta due centesimi!" demanded the cashier. (Twenty-three euro and ninety-two cents!)

I started sweating even more. I dug through my bag with shaky hands, gathered a twenty and a five-euro bill, and handed the money to her. As she counted, I held on to my breath for dear life, hoping that what I had handed over was the correct amount.

"Un'euro?" she asked. (One euro?)

Hearing her voice made my heart sink, and embarrassment washed over me.

"Mmmm … no," I muttered, hoping that my answer was sufficient and she would not ask me for anything else.

She seemed to roll her eyes, then printed out the receipt and handed it to me along with my change. I let out a sigh of relief, gathered my belongings, and stepped outside for some cigarette-smoke-tainted air. I always left that store feeling as though buying groceries was a crime. There always seemed to be another step that I could have taken, but I didn't know what step that was. The fear of bringing disappointment to Italians for not knowing their customs, and constantly embarrassing myself, forced me into hiding in my room until I felt brave enough to face the world again.

...

"I need more color in my life." I sighed.

"Girl, you are colorful," responded Courtney.

I was with Courtney—whom I had met thirty minutes prior—and Brenda—whom I had met before moving to Florence—at Piazzale Michelangelo. Brenda knew how to get there, so she took us after class one afternoon. From the viewpoint, I could see all of Florence's main attractions: the cathedral, Santa Croce Basilica, Piazza della Signoria, the Jewish synagogue, and the Arno River. In that moment, I caught a glimpse of Florence's beauty, and I felt dull in comparison—first to its people, and then to the actual buildings of the city. I had never seen such a constant crowd of elegantly dressed men, women, children, and teenagers. Nor had I ever seen such beautifully ornate buildings. My declaration was really me admitting that I needed more confidence in myself.

Later that night, when the sun went down, taking much of the heat with it, my roommates and I got dressed up to go to an event called Vogue's Fashion Night Out. My hair was pulled into a high bun, I was wearing a loosely fitted turquoise tank top, a long skirt with black-and-white tribal print, a black blazer, and grey sandals. The only makeup I wore was deep royal-purple lipstick. I felt decent, until we met up with all of our other friends and I noticed that most of the girls were wearing dresses.

"Everyone is so dressed up," I said to one of the girls named Amber.

"You look great. You always look great," Amber reassured me.

Being out amongst everyone made me feel like I was in a crowd that was waiting for a parade to start. There were people everywhere flooding the streets. We made our way from the carousel in Piazza della Repubblica all the way to a DJ and drink booth across from the Salvatore Ferragamo Museum. I was surrounded by people holding clear cups: Men wearing blazers clad in blue- or khaki-colored slacks and polished leather shoes, with their hair combed and slicked to the side. The women were wearing pumps, pencil skirts, and button-down blouses as they glided gracefully over the cobblestones. Even though everyone seemed to be dressed in a similar fashion, each person had their own unique style.

I noticed that every Italian seemed to possess a certain air of confidence and a carefree attitude. I envied the simple sexiness of the Italian women who surrounded me. To top it off, their Italian sounded like a song I wanted to learn the lyrics to.

I was standing near the bar when one of my friends walked over with an Italian guy. He was a friend of her friend, and he decided to hang out with us Americans for the night. I stood there not knowing what to say, until my insecurity finally formed a question.

"Why does everyone dress so good?" I asked.

"Yeah, like, are their closets full of expensive clothes? Or do they have a few really good items that they wear over and over?" asked my friend Lisa.

"Image is very important to most Italians," he said. "But mmm … it is not just about the dress, you know. It is how you can be. How to present yourself."

He went on to say that presentation starts in the mind first because how you see yourself, and what you think about yourself, is how you will present yourself.

His words spoke to my heart, telling me to change my mindset so that I could change how I saw life and myself. Who I am is not contingent upon what people think about me; it's about what I think of myself. If I constantly think that my clothes, hair, and how I look are not good enough, I will constantly compare myself and believe that what everyone else has is better than what I have.

I had been feeling so overwhelmed by the blaring fact that I did not fit in to Italian life. I was blundering my way through everything, barely getting by with the language and the cultural customs. I always felt judged. Looking back, you know, I wish I would've been able to just talk to myself and tell myself that it really was okay. So what if I constantly messed up or made a mistake. That was bound to happen since I was living in another country. So what if I didn't fit in. I wasn't meant to. I was meant to stand out. To constantly compare myself to every Italian who had been Italian and lived in that culture since birth was a grave mistake.

See, you can't compare yourself to someone who has been doing something way longer than you have. If you want to get to their level, that's admirable, and it will take time to get there. But to condemn yourself for not being on their level is just setting yourself up to fail. The reality is that color comes from within: from having confidence in yourself and letting that shine through.

Chapter Three

GET LOST, GET FOUND

I WAS THAT GIRL. The girl who would leave the market, take a wrong turn, keep walking and walking until I called on God for help, and then make it home an hour later than originally expected.

I was that girl who walked into a random cafè and ordered a tea I didn't want just to sit down and pretend like I was reading. All the while, I was really looking at my map. I was cursing at myself for not knowing where I was or how I would get home. I looked up to see a little girl with pigtails and a blue dress smiling at me. I mustered up everything to keep myself from letting tears run down my face. I took a deep breath, waved, and looked back at my map. The more I gazed down at my map, the closer she came to me.

"Ciao," I finally said.

I had the faintest, weakest smile on my face. My greeting made her smile and curl in on herself, as if she was too awestruck to think of a response.

"Ciao," said a deep voice off to my right. I looked over to see a man standing there.

"Ciao," I said again.

"Tu sei Americana?" he asked. (Are you American?) There was silence. "Parli Italiano?" he asked. (Do you speak Italian?)

I knew how to respond to his first question; I just didn't want to answer him. To his second question, I shook my head.

"Do you speak English?" he asked. I shook my head again.

"Parlez-vous français?" he asked yet again.

This time, I gave him the same weak smile I had given to his daughter. He also smiled back, his more sincere but with a hint of embarrassment and disappointment.

"Giulia, vieni," he said to the little girl. (Julia, come.)

I was once again alone to sulk and I looked down at the table. The image I saw caused my heart to skip a beat. I looked around hoping that man had not seen my book, and if he had, had he known I was lying to him about not speaking English? I quickly gathered my things and made my way to the door, trusting that I would somehow find my way home. Back in my empty room, I sat on my bed and buried my face in my hands. Moments later they were wet, and my breathing was so labored it was as if I was learning how to do it for the first time.

After getting lost so many times, I learned to just get used to it and to stop beating myself up for not knowing the way. This applies to life too. We are new to this life, just like I was new to Florence. We've never lived on Earth before, and sometimes we will make wrong turns or go down unfamiliar streets only to end up miles away from our destination.

Getting lost is a part of finding your way. Although I hated getting lost, I was able to see new parts of town, to practice my Italian by asking for help, and most importantly, to remember that I could always call on God and ask Him for help. I encourage you to be okay with getting lost. When you feel the anxiety rising up, stop, take a deep breath, and try to find your way again. You'll develop confidence in yourself. Sometimes, we don't need outside help, we just need to dig deep within and find the internal, built-in compass that is waiting to guide us to our final destination.

Chapter Four

MY MAIN DISTRACTION

I FELT SUFFOCATED BY the air inside of my room even though my window was wide open. I shooed a mosquito away that made a shrieking sound as it passed by my ear and went back to writing in my workbook. I leaned back in the plastic chair to stretch and give my eyes some rest. I looked outside my window and saw a man leaning over his balcony. He held his cellphone to his ear and held a glass of wine in the other hand. He was talking and smiling at the same time. I got up, stuck my head out of the window, and breathed in the thick, stagnant air. With the last inhale, my feet carried me back over to the table, and I sat down to finish my homework, certain that most of the answers were wrong. With a quick glance over my work, I closed the book and checked the time. *Time for me to make dinner and get ready for bed.*

There was still enough light outside to allow me to keep working in my room without turning the lamp on. Upon going back to my window, I saw that the man was still on his balcony. *He must be having a great conversation.* I leaned out of the window and grabbed one of the shutters. I was pulling it back to the center. I heard a deep voice with a hint of high-pitched eagerness proclaim, "Ciao!"

My head swiftly looked up to see the balcony man looking down at me.

"Ciao," I responded, and wanting to make my Italian teacher proud, I used the formal way to ask, "Come sta a Lei?" (How are you?)

"Sto bene. E tu?" he asked. (I'm good. And you?)

"Bene, grazie," I said. (Good, thanks.) I grabbed a hold of the other shutter.

"Tu sei una studentessa?" he asked. (Are you a student?) His question made me stop because it caught me off guard.

"Sì," I said. (Yes.) I was smiling as I tried to figure out what to say.

"Di dove sei?" He beat me to the punch. (Where are you from?)

At this point, my heart was racing out of pure eagerness to practice my Italian and pure fear of not knowing if I had remembered any of the lessons I was taught in class.

"Sono di California," I said. (I'm from California.)

"Ah, California." When he said, "California," I could tell he had never practiced saying that word out loud before. "Bello," he continued. (Nice.)

"Sì. Uh … buonanotte," I quickly said. (Yes. Uh … goodnight.)

"Buonanotte," he said.

Behind the shutters, my lips—as if acting separately from my brain—slid their corners up, revealing my teeth. My heart was pounding as I hummed and twirled around my room. I felt like I had won a competition that I had entered by chance.

...

The next day, I went to my Italian class at nine. I had class Monday through Friday, and on Fridays we would have a quiz for the material we learned during the week. This was my summer school before real classes started in November. I had been hoping to be in the advanced Italian class, especially since I had listened to an entire podcast teaching daily Italian phrases before moving to Italy. As I gazed down at the sentence "Write what you are here to study in Italian," which was on the test to gauge our knowledge of the language, my brain froze along with my pen.

I was placed in beginner Italian with a mix of students who majored in architecture, history, and English. My professor, Sophia, had a shy assertiveness about her. She walked in with her head down as she clutched her bag that was crammed into her armpit. Once her bag was placed on her desk, she stood there. She waited to speak once the voices quieted down. If she heard other voices while she was speaking, she would stop talking until there was silence. She never raised her voice or showed visible signs of annoyance.

"Allora, correggiamo i vostri compiti per casa. Pagina sessantasei," Sophia said. (Okay, let's correct your homework. Page sixty-six.)

I opened my workbook to the page I had been working on before having the conversation with the balcony man. The lesson for last night was important vocabulary words we needed to know when we went grocery shopping.

"'Portafoglio.' Cos'è quello?" Sophia asked.

I had gone through the trouble of defining most of the words in my workbook by memory, which meant that most of them were probably incorrect. Seeing the word "portafoglio"had made me chuckle a bit because the word seemed too obvious and directly translatable to English. As soon as I heard Sophia ask one of us to define that word, my hand shot up. I would take the bait for this word so that she wouldn't have to call on me when she wanted an answer for the words "negozio" (store), "mela" (apple), and "bustina" (bag).

"'Portafoglio' is 'portfolio' in English," I said.

Next to me, my friend Stephanie was giggling.

I narrowed my gaze at her. *What is so funny?*

"No," Sophia said before I could breathe a sigh of relief. I felt my face turn hot. "Wallet," she continued.

"Oh!" I proclaimed, feeling my armpits get wet.

"Everyone," Sophia's English was clear and assertive. "When you do homework please write the meaning." She held up her workbook and used her finger to "write" on the page. Then she continued, "It will help you to learn new words. It is important to practice your Italian with each other or ..." her voice trailed off, "you can watch films."

I looked over at Stephanie, who had her head turned to the side, and I faintly heard her giggling. I nudged her with my elbow.

"Okay," Sophia announced before rolling up her workbook and turning her back to us. The marker in her hand was hovering on the top right corner of the board.

"Dude, 'portfolio?'" Stephanie whispered. Her question caused me to giggle.

"Pagina sessantanove, esercizio ..." Sophia said, not really talking to us. (Page sixty-nine, exercise.)

When Sophia finished writing, she told us that this was our "compiti per casa" (homework) and we would go over it tomorrow. At noon, we were free to go.

To get over my embarrassment from class, I darted to the store near my house. I grabbed a baguette, basil, and tomatoes, not even caring if I ended up in the thin-red-haired cashier's line again. I was just eager to get home, cut the fresh baguette into bite-sized slices, top them with tomatoes soaked in balsamic vinegar, olive oil, and salt and then sprinkle chopped basil on top.

After I had finished grocery shopping, I was on the street right below my apartment. Everyone seemed to be out at this moment: women riding bikes, children running and holding hands, cars squeezing by, and dogs peeing on car wheels.

While walking through the crowd, I heard a voice say, "Ciao."

I looked up to see a man standing in front of me. I cocked my head to the side as I said, "Ciao," just to buy some time. The voice feigned familiarity and so did his features, vaguely. It's like I had unknowingly seen him at the grocery store.

Suddenly, my brain woke up and I said, "Ciao ... Ciao!"

"Come stai?" he asked. (How are you?)

"Bene. E tu?" I asked. (Good. And you?)

"Sto bene. Io vado a lavoro …" his voice trailed off.

"Lavoro?" … "lavoro?" What does that word mean? He was holding on to a bike, which was leaning against his side. When he spoke, I could see a full set of light-brown and yellow teeth. The two top center teeth were slightly facing each other like they were two friends having a casual conversation. He had acne scars on his cheeks, bags under his small brown eyes, a medium-sized nose, perfectly plump lips, and a beard that seemed to just be growing in. As he spoke, his body moved while his hands lifted and moved through the air like an actor telling a grand story.

He abruptly stopped speaking, so to act like I was paying attention, I quickly said, "Bene."

"Come ti chiami?" he asked. (What is your name?)

"Mi chiamo Kio," I said. (My name is Kio.)

"*Kio*, piacere. Sono Francesco," he said. (*Kio,* nice to meet you. I'm Francesco.)

"Francesco," I echoed. The sound of his name bounced around in my head.

"Che fai stasera?" he asked. (What are you doing tonight?)

"Io?" I asked. (Me?)

"Sì. Vuoi andare al bar con me?" he asked.

I stood there wondering what he said.

"Ti piace birra?" he asked. (Do you like beer?)

"No," I said, shaking my head.

"Va bene. Ti piace vino?" he asked. (That's okay. Do you like wine?)

"No," I admitted.

"Vero?" he asked, raising his eyebrows before continuing, "Cosa ti piace?" (Really? What do you like?)

"Io non bevo," I said. (I don't drink.)

"Non bevi?" He seemed shocked. (You don't drink?)

It's like he had never had to ask that question before.

"Io solo bevo acqua," I said. (I only drink water.) I hoped he would drop the issue.

Upon hearing that, he let out such an uninhibited form of laughter that most likely translated to, "How can you live in Italy and not drink wine?" Water to me was the most important liquid, while wine to an Italian was more important than water. With that, he found another way to ask me out by recommending we get gelato that night at eight. Gelato was music to my ears, so I agreed to meet him below our apartments later that evening.

At eight, I was standing in front of my apartment building's door. Looking to my left, right, and then up at his apartment didn't bring him out of hiding. A man standing across the street was smoking a cigarette. There was a subtle chill in the air that quickly passed, allowing the soft warm breeze to caress my bare arms. I crossed my arms so that either hand was clutching my triceps and began slowly twisting my torso from side to side. My heart started pounding as my eyes scanned my surroundings once again. I let out an exasperated sigh. *I'm only going to wait a little longer.* Before a little longer came, a familiar face appeared from behind a small wooden door. I felt myself starting to smile but forced my muscles to relax.

"Ciao," Francesco called as he crossed the street, not even bothering to look for a bicyclist or a Vespa. He reached me as I said, "Ciao," and before I could respond with anything else, I felt an abrasive texture rub my right cheek and then my left cheek. I giggled and looked down at my feet.

"Andiamo?" he asked. (Let's go?)

"Dove andiamo?" I asked. (Where are we going?)

...

We walked through Piazza Santa Croce then down a main street until we reached the Arno River. There were families out talking and strolling. The vibe of the city had settled down to a peaceful excitement. Cars and Vespas swept by as though being carried by a cloud. Or perhaps the cloud was actually carrying me. I felt like I was moving along with little effort on my part as we talked and walked around the city. At one point, he told me that he was thirty. *Really? If thirty looks like that, then I don't want to be that age.*

We ended up at the first *gelateria* I had gone to when I first arrived in Florence. It was named La Carraia, and they had the best gelato I had ever tasted. So, to say that I was impressed when he took me there would've been an understatement. As I tasted the creaminess of the ice cream, paired with the crunchiness of the dark chocolate cookies, I wanted to tell Francesco the story of how I had found this place. Words were bouncing around in my head, yet I lacked the ability to put them together into coherent sentences. Sitting in awkward silence until he broke it with a question became our norm for the evening. Surprisingly, the lack of conversation made for a peaceful tour around town as we walked down some more narrow streets. This time, when the view opened up, I saw the most beautiful building my eyes had ever seen. It was a perfectly rectangular, sand-colored building that looked like it belonged in a movie, not in real life. It sat on top of a slope as if looking down on everyone.

"Wow," I exclaimed, allowing my mouth to fall open.

"Questo è Palazzo Pitti," Francesco said to me. (This is Pitti Palace.)

I didn't care about the name; I just knew I liked it. We sat on the bare ground next to other couples. Francesco pulled out a pouch and rolled a cigarette and started smoking it. Instead of getting up and walking away, I stayed but made sure he blew the smoke away from my nostrils. After all, I was in Italy, and air and cigarette smoke were already competing for victory, so what could a little more cigarette smoke do? All I knew was that an Italian man was showing me attention, and I wanted the attention to fill my voids, so I brushed the red flags away and continued seeing him.

…

My careful footsteps were the only sounds echoing through my apartment. I quietly turned on the light and pulled back the small curtains. The garden and all of its pink, red, and white flowers were below. I opened the window and breathed in the fresh morning air. It was so peaceful, as if the morning hadn't yet risen from its slumber. I pulled myself back in, snuggled onto the couch, and took out my Bible and my journal. For much of my time in Florence, I would wake up at four in the morning to spend time with God.

In this particular moment, as I sat with Him, I wrote in my journal an important message that He was conveying to me: "Do not go into his apartment."

The words were clear and undeniable. I *knew* it was God telling me not to go into Francesco's apartment. It was *Him* because *I* wanted to get to know Francesco and go everywhere with him. God was warning me not to open the door to any kind of temptation. I wrote the warning down in my journal and kept it there as if it was just a friend, and not Almighty God, telling me to watch out. That night, Francesco and I went to a Neapolitan restaurant where I was able to order a dish called *pappa al pomodoro*. During one of our weekly meetings, my mentor, Chris, had told me about the dish and how it was bread soaked in a tomato sauce.

"That sounds gross!" I had exclaimed, sticking my tongue out.

"It's delicious. You should try it with olive oil drizzled on top," he had reassured me.

Since he had also recommended that I try pear juice (Wow! I don't even eat pears by themselves, but that juice was something else) and pistachio gelato, I figured that his taste in food was good. When the red-and-white mush was set before me, I drizzled olive oil on top. I scooped up a portion and wiped the spoon clean with my lips. I didn't really need to chew, as the bread and tomato soup dispersed over my taste buds.

The taste was comforting, subtle, and nothing to be heavily desired. In that moment, I was happy to be eating what Chris had recommended to me and also disappointed that it didn't live up to the hype. As I focused on eating, I was greeted by the awkward dead silence between Francesco and I once again. He was peeling apart some type of seafood, popping the edible parts into his mouth, and chewing. He also kept bouncing in his seat while looking around the restaurant instead of at me. I wanted to say anything to show that I knew how to have a conversation. Anything to impress the people around me whom I felt were staring at us. Their laughter, which seemed to be directed at us, sounded like mockery as to why this old, Italian man was with such a young, American girl.

To my relief, Francesco asked, "Buono?" (Good?)

"Sì, molto buono," I said. (Yes, very good.) I tried adding in the extra words to extend the talking time.

By the end of our meal, I felt full from the bread having expanded in my stomach and empty because of the lack of conversation. As we walked back towards our apartments all I could do was look around as my brain did backflips trying to land on one word I could say. My mind was always blank. It was as if a switch had been flipped so that no thought, not even an English one, entered my mind when I was around Francesco.

"Stai bene?" Francesco asked, interrupting my condemnation session. (Are you okay?)

"Oh … sì," I said.

We were now on our street—Borgo Allegri. I looked up at the 3rd floor window—my bedroom window—and saw the absence of light. *I don't want to go home.*

"Vuoi bere un tè con me?" Francesco asked. (Do you want to drink tea with me?) Maybe he saw the despair on my face.

"Oh, sì. Dove?" I asked. (Oh, yes. Where?)

"A casa mia," he said without hesitating. (At my house.)

Don't go into his apartment. I froze. I looked up at his apartment and noticed his balcony. *What was in there?* I had no reason not to trust Francesco; I just didn't know him. I also didn't want to be alone. I squeezed my tiny purse in search of my phone.

"Ummm… " I finally managed to push out.

"Solo per un po'. Vieni," he said. (It's only for a bit. Come.) He walked over to the entrance to his building before continuing, "Stai tranquilla, Kio." (It's okay, Kio.)

"Okay," I said, following him inside.

After hiking up what seemed like Mount Everest, I finally made it into his apartment. Once inside his place, there were still more stairs to go up, which took us to the dining room/kitchen area. I heard metals tinkling together and items being shuffled around.

"Kio." Francesco appeared. I walked closer to him and saw that he was standing in his kitchen holding a brown paper bag.

"Sì?" I asked, looking at him.

"Tè. Ti piace?" he asked, shaking the bag. (Tea. Do you like?) I nodded.

"Faccio io per io e te," he said. (I'll make it for you and me.)

"Okay."

I looked around and saw a chair near a window and a table full of pictures. I sat down, crossed my legs, and placed my hands on my knee. Francesco came over near me and turned on the radio with the press and flick of his index finger.

"Dadada," he sang out and returned back to the kitchen.

I watched him pour steaming water over the tea leaves that sat in a metal cage over a mug. He appeared to be whipping up a gourmet meal. I stood up to look out of the window. The view allowed me to look down at my bedroom window. The light was now on.

"Vivo qui," I said to Francesco. (I live here.) I was pointing and shaking my finger at my apartment building. He came over to look with me, doing so as if he had never seen my window from this view before.

"Bravissimo!" he exclaimed. (Amazing!) He lifted his hands up before returning back to the kitchen.

A few minutes later, he was carefully holding my cup of tea and tiptoeing it over to the dining room table. I got up and sat at the table. He joined me as I was studying the steaming brown liquid. I saw him put his cup to his lips and slightly tilt it. I did the same. The liquid tasted like stale dirt and old tree bark, so I asked for some honey. He brought over sugar instead. The sugar did very little to make the tea taste better. I pushed it aside. Just as I was getting comfortable, he said, "Fumo." (I'm going to smoke.)

I shrugged.

He was lost in another world as he smoked. When he let the smoke out, he seemed to be letting out a heavy sigh. Seeing him put the cigarette out was my cue to get up and stand by him. He looked up at me. I caught him in mid thought, but he smiled at me.

"Ciao. Hai finito?" he asked. (Hey. Are you finished?)

"Sì," I said.

"Sì!" he exclaimed.

I laughed, then yawned. He got up and went into the kitchen. I was examining the pictures on the wall near the window. There was a picture of a younger Francesco standing in front of a large "M" shaped mountain. He had a big smile on his face and was leaning against a railing. *Where is he at? I haven't seen a place like that in Florence. Or maybe he could be –*

My body jerked forward. I felt his body press up against my back as his hands moved across my belly and clutched my waist. His lips were kissing the side of my neck.

"Oh, Kio," he whispered.

I gasped and without thinking, I grabbed his hands, prying them apart and turned around to face him.

"Siamo amici," I said, pushing him away. (We are friends.)

"Scusa," he said. (Sorry.)

He placed his hand over his lips, similar to the way someone covers their mouth after they let out a burp.

"Io vado ora," I said. (I'm going now.)

"Okay, scusa, Kio." (Okay, I'm sorry, Kio.)

…

My eyes followed the greens, yellows, and browns outside the bus window. Chatter filled the air. I blocked out the noise with melodies of the band Bon Iver flowing through my earphones. My thoughts were stuck on last night's blunder with Francesco. I couldn't fault him, only myself for going into his apartment in the first place. The fact that communication with him was difficult and nearly impossible wasn't helping our situation. *Did I not make it clear to him that we were friends?* I was able to sit with my thoughts, even taking out my journal to write things down. This bus would be my post for the next few hours since I was on a field trip with my school.

My classmates and I had just left a picturesque town called Arquà Petrarca where we had strolled around with Fabio and Professor Leo Fontana. We had gone to Petrarch's house and saw his mummified cat that looked more like a block of cement. I was more interested in the scenery. The clouds in the town looked like soft pillows nestled into the light and medium blue sky as they sailed back towards two cone-shaped mountains. Covering all of the land were greens: fields of green grass; rows of vineyards; and groups of billowy, round trees with pomegranates hanging from the vines. Joining the gathering was a blue body of water. In the middle of it all was a small rectangular home with a pastel pink roof. When two Italian men dressed in their biking attire rode by us and said, "Ciao," the clouds from the sky swooped down and lifted me up. I was absolutely in awe.

When we were dropped off in Verona and saw the wall at Juliet's house covered with letters, I was also in awe. Even when my friends Brent and Stephanie and I got lost trying to find our group, I was happy because I allowed myself to enjoy the moment. I even enjoyed the simple action of bending over to put my lips to a stream of water to quench my thirst in Venice. I was able to effortlessly maneuver through what seemed like millions of pedestrians as Leo Fontana led us to an Italian restaurant that no tourists knew about. When I ordered my food, I, unlike everyone else who said, "Voglio avere la lasagna," (I want to have the lasagna) said, "Prendo la lasagna." (I'll take the lasagna.) Hanging out with Francesco was helping me to feel more confident in trying new Italian phrases.

When our boat sped away from Venice, I got splashed with water from the sea. I made light of it because I had finally felt like myself again. The minute we arrived back in Florence, I wanted to share my excitement with Francesco. It was well after nine o'clock in the evening on a Sunday. I wanted to sleep, even though I had homework to do. I instead sat on the steps of Santa Croce with Francesco. He pulled something out of his pocket and handed it to me.

"Cosa c'è?" I asked. (What is it?)

"È un dizionario per te," he said. (It's a dictionary for you.)

"Grazie," I said, smiling.

Then he pulled out an iTouch, much like mine, and tapped on an app that opened a translator. We spent time talking through the app. Somehow, my conversation of how beautiful the places were that I had just seen turned into what Francesco did for work, and then he mentioned how he could help dye my hair after school around four o'clock the next day. With that, I bid Francesco good night, went back home, and climbed into my bed.

...

By four o'clock, I was already seated on a concrete bench on the right side of Piazza Santa Croce. I was at the place where Francesco said we would meet and where I was sure to get a Wi-Fi signal on my iTouch. The activity around me was normal. The African dudes were walking up to couples and waving a rose in the women's faces. Others were throwing around fluorescent bouncy balls and blowing whistles. The others stood beside white sheets that had knockoff designer bags on top of them.

By 4:15 p.m., Francesco still hadn't come, so I decided to log on to the Wi-Fi and check my email. To my surprise, there was an email from him. Reading the Italian words sent my breath down to the pit of my stomach. In fact, I might've stopped breathing altogether. Anger, sadness, disappointment, and betrayal sat next to me on the bench. One by one, they began pulling me into their clutches.

"Mi dispiace (I'm sorry) … Ho dimenticato (I forgot) … Con il mio cugino (With my cousin)." I sat on the bench blinking and raising my eyebrows to cover up how visibly annoyed I was. I didn't want anyone to see me cry, so I got up and dragged my feet back to my room.

The tears didn't need any encouragement to slide freely down my face. I felt abandoned and rejected. I couldn't understand why he would do that to me. "Stupid," I said and grabbed my laptop. I sent my mom an email, telling her that I was sad, feeling lonely, and that I loved her and that I was taking a walk up to Piazzale Michelangelo. I closed my laptop and left my apartment.

I held back tears as I stomped all the way to my destination. The city looked like it was covered by a blue veil. The spotlights that illuminated the main attractions shown even brighter than usual. Florence was more beautiful than I had ever seen it. The beauty of the city was begging for my attention. It said to me, "Look at where you are, Kio. Don't let that man steal your joy." I stayed up there until the urge to wring Francesco's neck disappeared.

Back at my apartment, I checked my email and didn't see one from my mom. The next day before I went to school, I checked my email again. *I wonder why mom hasn't responded.* I scoffed. There was an email from Francesco. He was apologizing again. All I wanted to do was curse him out. I instead gathered my backpack and went to school.

As soon as Sophia said, "Ciao. Ci vediamo a domani" (Bye. See you all tomorrow), I darted out of the classroom with a mission to get some fresh produce from Sant'Ambrogio Market. As I was walking back home, still very near the market, a dude on his bike stopped in front of me. I stopped too.

"Ciao. Come stai?" said Francesco. (Hey. How are you?)

I shrugged.

"Che fai?" he asked. (What are you doing?)

I rolled my eyes, looked down at my bags then up at him, and let out an exasperated sigh.

"Kio, io faccio lavoro adesso. Dopo, vuoi mangiare pranzo con me?" (Kio. I'm working right now. After, do you want to eat lunch with me?)

"Perché?" I asked. (Why?)

"Cosa?" He frowned and leaned forward. (What?)

"Lo sai!" I screamed at him. (You know!)

"Scusa, *Kiooo*. Non ti volevo fare male," he said, as if pleading a case.

The only word I understood was "scusa," and he was frowning again. I looked up and saw people glaring at us. *What could they be thinking?*

"Kio, vado io, scusa. Sto lavorando, però per favore, mangiamo insieme a casa mia all'una," he said as he started to peddle away. (Kio, I have to go, sorry. I am working, but please, let's eat together at my house at one.)

"Luna?" I asked, confused as to why he was talking about the moon. (*Luna* in Italian means "moon" and also means "one" in reference to time, which I didn't know back then).

"Alle uno," he said, looking back at me. (At one.)

He held up his stubby index finger and rode away before I could even agree. Of course he knew I would go. I had already explored most of the city, so all of the excitement of being in a new town was slowly fading away. Life was becoming normal and uneventful. I also didn't hang out with my friends too much because they were busy art students.

…

At one, I was staring at a table set with plates and utensils. The breeze was blowing the multicolored tablecloth. From where I stood, the dome of the cathedral was perfectly centered in front of me. I had the desire to snap an image of the scenery and post it on Instagram. I took the picture and decided against posting it because I didn't want anyone to ask me where I was. Our lunch for the day was chicken strips, lettuce, and olive oil mixed with ketchup and paprika.

"Buon appetito," said Francesco.

I had only been chewing for a minute before Francesco broke the silence with, "Sei andata in Piazzale Michelangelo ieri sera?" (You went to Piazzale Michelangelo last night?)

I kept chewing at the same pace. I didn't want to show that I was alarmed by his question, even though I definitely was. Meanwhile, my brain was asking how the heck he knew that?

"Sì. Era bellissimo," I said in my calmest tone. (Yes. It was so beautiful.)

"Perché sei molto triste?" he asked, looking me right in my eyes. (Why are you so sad?)

"Umm… non lo so," I whispered, looking away. (Umm … I don't know.)

"Manca tua mamma?" (Do you miss your mom?)

"Certo," I said. (Of course.)

I was now glaring at him, hoping his intentions would reveal themselves to me. "Umm… perché … perché parli così?" I demanded. (Umm … why … why are you talking like this?)

"Ho ricevuto il tuo email," he said. (I received your email.)

I swallowed hard after hearing the word "email." *No wonder why mom had never responded.*

"Well, I was sad because you abandoned me. We planned to meet, and then you changed your mind at the last minute," I said.

I looked at him and waited for him to respond. He just stared at me, chuckled, pulled out his iTouch, and handed it to me. I typed what I had just said into the translation app. Once he finished reading what I had typed out, his body seemed to come alive with understanding.

"Ahhh, Kio, scusami. Mi dispiace. Non volevo farti male. Mi sono sbagliato," he began.

I stared at him and drained all the expression from my face.

"Oh okay. Un attimo," he said, taking his iTouch back. (One second.)

I read his paragraph. He was apologizing to me as sincerely as a translation app could get across. This is how most of my conversations with him went. As time went on, my Italian did improve, and we didn't need to use the app as much. But, if I wanted to have a deep, intellectual conversation with him, I simply couldn't.

…

I had never been in love before. My "love" life consisted of having flings with guys. We'd make out, heavy pet, and then go our separate ways. Even though doing those things gave me butterflies and a sense of connection to the person, it was never a deep connection that I knew would last. I'd never built a relationship on friendship or on purely getting to know someone for who they were. It seemed that when a guy approached me, it was always because I looked good to them. It's not like they were trying to get to know me for me.

I was never taught what guys were up to or how to avoid their games. Nor was I taught how to value myself and my body and to slow down rather than to give too much too soon. I eventually learned those lessons, but those lessons weren't instilled in me when I needed them the most. Instead of taking things slowly with Francesco, I allowed my desire to be loved to turn into desperation. I hadn't even known him for two months, yet I poured my heart out to him in a letter, written on a white-and-pink trimmed piece of paper that was taken from my journal. In my poor Italian grammar, I told him that he was special and that I was happy to know him. I placed the letter into my bag, got up from my desk, opened up my window, and stuck my head outside. It had just rained. The air smelt like wet pavement instead of cigarette smoke. I closed my eyes and took in slow, deep breaths. I opened my eyes and I looked to my right and saw numerous white tents and people gathering around the tents. Out of nowhere, Francesco appeared on his balcony. He stretched his arms towards the sky, then he looked down at me.

"Oh, ciao! Cosa fai?" He asked. (Oh, hey! What are you doing?)

"Niente, che cosa successo?" I asked. (Nothing, what's happening?)

"It's an antique market that happens every month." Eva's voice surprised me from behind. I pulled myself back inside to say, "Oh, okay, cool," and then leaned back outside. I locked eyes with Francesco, and we both smiled.

"Vuoi andare al caffè con me?" he asked. (Do you want to go to a coffee shop with me?)

"Sì!" I exclaimed, wanting to say "Yes" as soon as he said "Vuoi." *Of course I want to be with you ... Did you even have to ask? I would've done anything with you.*

"Bello. Andiamo. Incontriamo laggiù," he said and then pulled himself back inside. (Great. Let's go. We'll meet below.)

I made sure the letter was in my bag, grabbed my umbrella, and said, "Bye," to Eva. We walked past the antique market where everyone seemed to be more focused on the items than on the fact that another torrential downpour could start at any moment. Just being next to Francesco was enough for me. We walked while occasionally looking at each other to see who could smile the brightest. We were just crossing the street. I saw dark circles forming on the ground and felt taps on my head.

"Piove!" Francesco cheerfully shouted. (It's raining!)

"Oh no!" I exclaimed.

He took off running as he fumbled to get his umbrella open. I popped mine open and set my feet into motion—not thinking, not even reacting, just being. Our feet pounded against the pavement before puddles had the chance to form. When we made it underneath shelter, Francesco let out a big, "Phew," laughed, and walked towards a door that was attached to a building off of a courtyard. Something familiar about the place appealed to my memory. I stopped to read the words printed in block lettering on the red wall. "Caffè Letterario," the words read. It struck me that I had wandered into this very courtyard just a few weeks prior. There hadn't seemed to be anything going on, and I definitely hadn't seen *this* door before, so I had walked away.

It felt like Francesco was taking me to a secret underground party somewhere. He was already talking to the guy at the register as I walked in. He turned to look back at me when he heard me come inside.

"Kio, vuoi un tè?" he inquired. (Kio, do you want tea?)

"Mmm …" I said as I walked closer, standing next to Francesco to look at the menu. "Oh! Cioccolata caldo per favore," I said. (Oh! Hot chocolate please.)

"Un'espresso e un ciocco …" Francesco's voice trailed off. (An espresso and a hot choco …)

I turned away to look around the place.

"Bello, eh?" Francesco said, walking by me.

He descended a few stairs and sat at a table in a dimly lit part of the cafè. As I sat down, Francesco was smiling again as if he was thinking of something funny.

"Che divertente! Wow!" he remarked. (How fun! Wow!)

I smiled. I wanted to say something other than my canned response of, "Sì," to literally everything he said.

Without even trying, the phrase, "Sono d'accordo," slipped off my tongue. (I agree.)

I stared at Francesco with wide eyes. I had just stunned myself.

"Brava! Il tuo Italiano è molto bene," Francesco remarked. (Amazing! Your Italian is very good.)

"Grazie." I felt my cheeks get warm.

"Oh, scusa," he said.

He got up suddenly to walk back over to the counter. As I sat alone, I took the note out of my bag and set it on Francesco's side of the table. In another room, beyond an alcove, sat a couple. Picture frames hung all around. Darkness was the most prominent element in the room, yet it wasn't the palpable darkness that one fears. It was the darkness that belonged: a darkness that sets the mood.

"Prego," Francesco said. (Here you go.)

He placed my hot chocolate on the table and then jerked back when he saw the piece of paper sitting there.

"Che c'è?" he asked. (What is this?)

"Una lettera ho scritto per te," I said. (A letter I wrote for you.)

He picked his espresso up, put the small ceramic cup to his lips, and quickly tilted the cup before placing it back down in order to unfold the paper. His eyes moved from left to right, scanning my words. I wasn't expecting anything. I was just wanting to give a letter to a friend. I sat sipping my hot chocolate as I watched him read the letter. He sniffed, wiped his eyes with his finger, folded the paper, and tucked it into his jacket's pocket. His eyes were glistening. I smiled at him.

"Wow Kio, grazie. Tu sei davvero un angelo," he said softly. (Wow, Kio, thank you. You are truly an angel.)

. . .

The more we hung out, doing our best to string some sort of conversation together with the help of dictionaries and translators, the more I felt my heart leaning into his and ignoring the blatant red flags. Not only did he smoke, but he could also drink an entire bottle of wine in one sitting. He drank beer too, which was a beverage I thought Italians didn't drink. I would always express to him my dislike for that, yet I stayed put. One day, I was sitting on a bench underneath an awning with Francesco. I saw him digging in his pocket, take out his phone, look at it, and then put it to his ear.

"Pronto?" He said. (Hello?)

He got up to pace around as he spoke a few feet away from me.

I sat there, watching him, and when I got bored, I looked at my feet that were clad in black boots. I looked up to see the couple I had seen a handful of times walking their black Great Dane look-alike. Suddenly, the dog decided to release his bowels, and a big pile of poop plopped to the pavement. I grimaced yet never turned away. I didn't even look away as I watched the man take two hands covered in plastic bags to scoop up some of the mess. He had to come back to get rid of the rest of it. Dogs in Florence pooped on the streets and peed on car tires or buildings. I was advised to always look down when I walked. Thankfully, I never stepped in anything, but I did have classmates who did. As I was snickering to myself, Francesco reappeared at my side. He sighed before sticking his phone back into his pocket.

"Allora," he said. (Alright.)

His voice was so monotone it sounded like he had just woken up from a nap. I looked at him and waited for him to continue his sentence.

"Hai fame?" he asked. (Are you hungry?)

Duh, is that even a question? I'm always hungry! No matter how many baguettes or pizzettas I shove into my face, my stomach is never satisfied.

For some reason, I shook my head, as if to say "No," which prompted him to walk in a direction away from me.

"Okay?" I muttered to myself as I rolled my eyes and followed him anyway, like a lost puppy. "Come stai?" I asked when I caught up to him.

"Ah, bene. Tutto bene," he said. (Ah, good. Everything is good.)

He gave me the fakest smile I'd ever seen him produce, like he had stolen it from my lips. I put my arm through his, and when he didn't pull away, I felt like he was okay with me. We strolled over to the Ponte Vecchio, which was full of tourists checking out the jewelry stores that lined the bridge.

"Kio." I felt Francesco moving his arm away to dig into his pocket, so I moved mine away too. "Puoi fare una foto di me?" he asked. (Can you take a photo of me?)

"Sì, certo. Dove?" (Yes, sure. Where?)

"Qui," he said, standing near a wall. (Here.)

I turned the screen towards him after snapping a few pictures. He used his hand to cup the screen.

"Sono brutto," he said matter-of-factly. (I'm ugly.)

"What? Non è vero," I said, frowning. (That's not true.)

"Sì. Bruttissimo," he said, pouting. (Yes. Really ugly.)

"Tu sei bello," I said. (You are handsome.)

"No, sei bella. Sono brutto." (No, you're beautiful. I'm ugly.)

He wasn't the most attractive person ever, he was just Francesco. Whenever he would talk about himself like that or look upset, I did my best to lift his spirits. Some days I was able to do so, and he seemed to be back to his normal vibrant self. But, other days, doing so resulted in me feeling drained and hopeless just like him. Most days, something just didn't feel right, yet I couldn't put my finger on it. At the time, I didn't see any red flags. Either way, I kept ignoring them. Not just that, but I began bleaching the obvious red flags when he told me that he was actually forty, not thirty, had been married, was now divorced, and had a daughter who was one year younger than me.

Why did I bleach the red flags? Because I was being dumb and desperate. I was also afraid of being abandoned, and it was like I wanted to save him. I wanted to help pull him out of the funk he kept falling into. He did seem nice to me and didn't seem to disrespect me. The more I hung out with him, the more I found myself lusting after him.

One night as we watched a movie called "The Last Kiss," I made a move and kissed him. From that day on, our relationship turned physical in terms of heavy petting and making out. We never had sex because I wanted to save that for my husband. When we weren't being physical, we were talking, he was cooking for me or teaching me how to make homemade *ragù*, taking me on picnics, helping me with my homework, or taking me on biking and walking adventures around Florence.

Being with him was thrilling. Yet, the thrills were never enough to compensate for the utter lows I also felt with him. The color I wanted in my life was slowly fading to black. The more I hung out with him, the more energy I felt being drained from my soul. He always seemed to be faking his happiness. Whenever I caught him in the middle of a thought, he would be looking off into the distance with a look of despair on his face.

…

I had been feeling down because I had just gotten news of my uncle dying. I texted Francesco to ask him if he was free. I just wanted a hug and wanted to sulk in his company. He told me it was okay to come over.

"Ciao," I called out, pushing the front door open. I was greeted by silence.

"Francesco?" I walked to his bedroom and peered inside. He was standing in the middle of his room whimpering.

"Che successo?" I asked. (What happened?)

I walked up to him and embraced him. I had never seen any man in my life cry like that.

"Voglio… voglio morire," he managed to get out. (I want to die.) "Non voglio vivere più." (I don't want to live anymore.)

I let go and stepped back. His face was so swollen and red, it looked like he had been slapped using an open palm numerous times.

"Vuoi morire? Perchè?" I asked. (You want to die? Why?) I scratched my forehead and rubbed my eyes.

"Non voglio vivere più," he said. (I don't want to live anymore.)

I held my hand up at him and scoffed.

"Wait, you want to die? Il mio zio è morto!" I exclaimed, throwing up my hands. (My uncle died!) "Lui voleva vivere ma ora lui non può vivere più. Tu vivi. Perchè voglio morire?"

I raised my voice. (He wanted to live but now he can't live anymore. You're alive. Why do you want to die?)

I felt my face get hot. My heart was pounding faster than normal and I was glaring at Francesco and shaking my head.

"Beatrice," he said, sniffling.

"Chi è Beatrice?" I asked. (Who is Beatrice?)

He told me she was his ex-girlfriend. She had broken up with him just before I moved into my apartment. She had been living with him and would stay home all day doing nothing while he went to work. After using him for sex and shelter, she told him she didn't love him and then left him for another man. One day, she had seen us out together. This sight triggered some sort of jealous rage in her because she then kept calling him to harass him. I placed my hand over my mouth. All along, I thought he had been taking business calls. She really only seemed to call when we were out together. Was she watching us?

After hearing all of this, I made it my mission to help him get his mind off of Beatrice. I wanted to be his savior. Whether or not I could see it clearly at the time, it was obvious that he didn't care about me. Even though all of this drama and his sadness were slowly draining all of my life and vibrancy, I liked having him around as a distraction. He was a drug—I knew he was bad for me, but I needed the highs to get me through.

…

My professor for my Italian conversation class was a hippie-looking lady named Chiara. Her normal speaking voice was just above a whisper. She wore colorful skirts and jewelry and was very animated in her speech and gestures. Her language was so creative that she came up to me, and looking at my hair perched on top of my head, remarked, "I tuoi capelli sono come un nido per gli uccelli." (Your hair is like a nest for birds.) Her comment was so unlike anything anyone had ever said about my hair that I just laughed.

After remarking about my hair, she asked the class if we missed our families. Hearing that pulled at my heart strings more than her comment about my hair. I started tearing up, which I found to be unusual. When I had been at school back in the states, I had missed my family, but it had never brought me to tears. Missing home back there had always been salvaged by talking to my mom. If I did want to go back home, it was easy to carpool, or I would get on a plane and be home in an hour. Getting home from Italy was more complex with the distance, making me realize that things cannot always be as easy as I wish them to be. After class, I went to visit one of the administrative staff members.

"Hi, Rose. Can I talk to you?" I said, standing in the doorway. I was fully prepared to start bawling my eyes out and tell her that I wanted to go home.

"Sure, of course, Kio. Come in."

I sat down at the chair right across from her. I could see the computer screen reflecting in her glasses.

"What's going on?" she asked.

"In class, Chiara asked us if we missed our families. I started feeling sad because I miss my mom. I would usually go home for Thanksgiving." I felt my eyes getting hot.

"I understand. It can be tough not being able to go home. What are you going to do for Thanksgiving?"

"Umm, I'm just going to a small gathering with my roommates. They're architecture students."

"Oh, right. Eva and Lucy?"

"Yeah. They invited me to go to their friends' place."

"Are you going to cook anything?"

"Yeah." I sighed. "I'm going to make macaroni and cheese. I hope it's good."

She told me how delicious that sounded and that I should go to the store, get the ingredients, and start making it to take my mind off of things. She then told me how she was spending Thanksgiving in another town at a cottage with her family. Her voice and her stories calmed me down.

"That sounds awesome. I hope you have lots of fun," I said, doing my best to sound enthusiastic.

"I hope you enjoy your Thanksgiving as well. Go along to the market," she said.

"Thanks, I will."

As I was getting up from the chair she added, "Keep smiling so that the world can see your beautiful smile."

After leaving her office, I went to the store and bought the ingredients needed for the mac and cheese, then I went home and Skyped my mom. At the end of my Skyping session, Eva's friend came over to use our oven so that she could start cooking her portion of the Thanksgiving meal for the next day. All of us were having a great time talking and helping her prepare the food. About thirty minutes after she came, another friend joined us to help us cook.

On Thanksgiving morning, Eva made eggs Benedict for my house plus her two friends from the previous day. We were together all day cooking. My apartment was filled with scents of butter, onions, sugar, and cinnamon. Besides the large portion of macaroni and cheese I made, we had pumpkin pie, stuffing, mashed potatoes, a brussels sprouts dish, and homemade cranberry sauce. We toted our bounty over to their friends' apartment. Each of the twelve people that attended the dinner party brought a dish to share, so there was more than enough food to go around. There were even enough leftovers that samples from each dish were sent home with each household. I felt so welcomed, even though I was meshing with people who already knew one another very well.

Around this time, a Christmas market had sprung up in Piazza Santa Croce. I braved the cold nights to hang out with my friends as they drank spiced wine and I ate German sweets. The upcoming Christmas holiday meant that most of my schoolmates were traveling with friends to go visit new countries. Courtney and Brenda had already booked time in Paris without me, so that was out. I didn't want to travel anywhere alone, nor did I want to stay in Florence, even though my friend Alex said that she was staying behind. Well, my desire to experience a real Italian Christmas ended up being too strong to decline Francesco's invitation to go to Naples with him and his family. When my classmates would ask me what I was doing for the break, I would just tell them that I was going to Naples with a friend. No further questions, please.

Since Francesco's only mode of transportation was a bike, we used a rideshare to take the five-hour trip down to Naples. The guy driving kept asking how we knew each other because he couldn't seem to fathom why an older Italian guy was with a young Black girl. I couldn't fathom it either, yet there we were. Francesco's response of "Lei é un'amica della familia," (She's a friend of the family) was enough to get him to stop asking questions but not enough to keep him from eyeing us in the rearview mirror as he was driving.

Meeting Francesco's family wasn't all that awkward for me. What was awkward was learning that we were sharing a room in his parents' home—separate beds though. This meant that I had zero privacy and really would be around him all day every day. When we weren't together eating a large meal at his parents' house, we were out visiting his friends and family and eating full meals at their houses. Everyone I met was polite to me. I met Francesco's sister and her husband and his older brother and his wife.

Then, I met his loud cousin who owned a shoe shop. As soon as we walked into the shop, his cousin greeted me by pulling me in and kissing me on both cheeks. As our cheeks touched, I caught a glimpse of a figure standing behind him. Once he was done grabbing me, I was able to see that the figure was one of the most beautiful women I'd ever seen in my life. He introduced her as Arianna. She said, "Ciao," to me, and I greeted her back and stood there as Francesco and his cousin spoke in a dialect known as "Napoletano." I couldn't understand anything that they were saying. They stepped outside, leaving me alone with Arianna.

She kept staring at me, looking me up and down as though she were trying to size me up. I gave her a barely there smile and looked around at all of the shoes that lined the walls up to the ceiling. I could hear and see Francesco and his cousin. Just as I was about to walk out to go join them, his cousin came inside. He said something in Napoletano to Arianna, gave her some money, and went back through a door that opened up into a garage.

"Vieni con me," she said. (Come with me.)

She looked at me and walked towards the door. I looked over at Francesco and saw his lips say, "Va bene." (It's okay.)

As we walked down the street, Arianna asked me where I was from, what I was doing in Italy, and most importantly, how old I was.

"Ho ventuno anni," I said. (I am twenty-one years old.)

"Quello uomo con cui sei stata, quanti anni ha?" she asked. (That man that you were with, how old is he?)

She took my hand and placed it on her forearm so that we were walking arm in arm. I paused for a second, taking everything in. She had seemed so cold towards me when we first arrived. Now she was holding me like we were best friends.

"Umm …" I stammered, trying not to alarm her so that she wouldn't let me go. "Lui ha quaranta anni," I admitted, avoiding her eyes. (He is forty years old.)

I felt her squeeze my hand before saying, "Perché tu stai con un'uomo come lui? Lui è vecchio. Sei molto bella e giovane." (Why are you with a man like him? He's old. You're beautiful and young.)

"Mmm …" I was doing my best to formulate a response.

Anything I would've said would've sounded foolish and illogical. Suddenly, I felt her pull me towards her and into a grocery store. She walked down the aisles, dodging people and picking up items, yet didn't once let go of me. She handed me two bags filled with white balls and clear liquid while she held on to other items as we stood in line. The only time she let go of me was to pay the cashier. With the change in her hand and the plastic bag on her arm, she took my hand again as we walked back to the shop.

She told me about her fiancé and how wonderful he was. They were getting married next year, and she invited me to the wedding. I had always dreamt about attending a wedding in another country. With great pain, I declined her invitation, telling her that I would be leaving to go back home in a few months.

When we made it back to the shoe shop, she put the grocery bag onto a desk. I sat down on a metal chair off to the side. After putting the money in one of the drawers, she came and sat next to me. She again told me that I was beautiful and that I deserved better than Francesco. She also told me that I was sweet and kind. I felt a rush of emotions welling up inside me, and I wanted to cry. It's like she was an angel sent down to help me see my worth and realize that what I was doing wasn't who I was. She took my hand again and held it as it rested on her knee. She looked into my eyes and smiled at me just as Francesco and his cousin were walking back into the shop. His cousin said something really loudly, walked over to the desk, grabbed the bag, and then walked back out.

"Kio, andiamo con lui," Francesco said. (Kio, we're going with him.)

Arianna was pulling me up, before I could register what Francesco had said to me, and was pulling me in and kissing me on both cheeks.

"Ciao, Kio. È stato un bello piacere. Deviamo continuare a parlare. Hai Facebook?" she asked. (Bye, Kio. It was a beautiful pleasure. We need to keep talking. Do you have Facebook?)

Francesco walked back out, allowing us to have our moment. After exchanging information, I said to her, "Grazie mille, Arianna. Sei una bella donna. Grazie per le tue parole. Sei gentile. Grazie." (Thank you so much, Arianna. You are a beautiful woman. Thank you for your words. You are kind. Thank you.)

We embraced like we had known each other for years. I walked out the door to go convene with Francesco and his cousin. Once I was out the door, I turned back to wave at Arianna. She smiled and blew me a kiss.

...

I had finally gotten what I wanted: to be around Francesco nonstop, and it was driving me insane. His jokes were no longer funny, and his real personality was starting to come out. One day, he wanted to take me on an adventure to go to the famous pizzeria in Naples. We were sitting in the underground train station. A man walked by and a cloud of cigarette smoke followed him. Francesco had the nerve to cough and wave the smoke away from his face. I glared at him and said, "Ma perché? Fumi." (But why? You smoke.)

He schooled me on the fact that *his* cigarettes were different. See, since he rolled his, *his* were pure. *That* man was smoking a cigarette with other bad things added to it. My blood boiled. I had an attitude the entire time we were out that day, even as I ate my entire delicious pizza, and then pretty much every day after that. Something about him seemed more off than usual. He seemed more agitated and easily angered.

I really got a wake-up call on Christmas Eve. I was sitting at the table with Francesco, his mom, his dad, and his older brother. We had just gotten done eating a full meal, and because it was Christmas Eve, his mom wanted to light one of the candles as some sort of religious ritual. As soon as that fire hit that wick, I could see Francesco stewing in his seat. She carried out her ritual and then blew the candle out. I saw Francesco's hand pick the candle up and start shaking it at his mom as he said something to her in Italian. I caught a few words of him complaining about her Catholic beliefs. As he raised his voice, she raised hers, and they got into a heated argument that, in my mind, was uncalled for.

I sat there, picking up not so much on the words that were said but the energy that was in the room. His father and brother both sat in silence. Francesco stormed away to go smoke a cigarette in the bathroom, even though his mom had asked him before not to do any of that. I shook my head, rolled my eyes, and got up to go sit on the balcony outside the kitchen.

I took the deepest breath I had taken since being in Naples. I finally let my shoulders relax and my mind wander back over the past few months that I had spent—not just in Florence—but with Francesco. He had been the first older man that I had been with. Calling what we had a relationship probably would've been far-fetched. We had more of an involvement. I was still new to all of this, yet I knew that how I was being treated wasn't right. I knew that the knots in my stomach didn't have a place there all the time. I felt such a weight on me. It was as if all of my poor decisions were finally calling me out and disciplining me for ignoring the red flags. I also saw that there was a way out. The string tugging on my heart to pull me away was still attached. All I had to do was get up, follow the string, and not look back.

The sun had started to warm the side of my face when I heard the sound of the screen door dragging open. Francesco appeared at my side.

"Ciao," he said with a smile.

"Ciao," I said, not even caring to move my tongue or even try to say the word.

"Che c'è?" he asked. (What's up?)

I put my hand up to block the sun so that I could look him in the eyes. My heart was racing, and I felt my stomach starting to knot up. I ignored my feelings and let the words roll off of my tongue.

"Io vedo chi sei e non mi piace," I said, without stumbling over my words. (I see who you are, and I don't like it.)

It was as if I was actually looking at myself and saying those words.

He paused for a moment and said, "Eh? Chi sono?" (Eh? Who am I?)

Although subdued, I heard the irritation in his tone as he asked the question. If someone had said my words to *me*, I would've allowed all of my irritation to be on full display. I want to say that my Italian fluency kicked into high gear and I was able to give him a rundown of every moment that proved my point, but that didn't happen. I did end up telling him about the episode with his mom and how ridiculous it was for him to get so mad. To my surprise, he agreed. Sadly, that still wasn't enough for me. I wanted out of there.

The day for me to leave Naples finally came after eating all day on Christmas, experiencing an explosion at his sister's house from a stove-top coffee maker, being jolted around by an earthquake, and then eating all day again at his brother's mansion on New Year's Eve. When the rideshare, filled with three college guys, came to pick me up, I was ready to leave and never look back. Francesco bid me farewell until he returned to Florence and watched as the car took me away.

I sat in silence as I looked out the window until the guy sitting next to me interrupted my thoughts.

"Quello è il tuo uomo?" he asked. (Is that your man?)

I paused for a moment to think about my response. Finally, I said, "No. Io sono solo un'amica della sua familia." (No. I'm only a friend of his family.)

…

Being back in Florence and away from Francesco completely for the first time in months was the medicine my soul needed in order to gain some real insight and strength to fully cut ties. It took me another month or so to fully break away from him. I even received an email from Beatrice berating me for getting with him because of his age. I saw them together twice. One of the times, I was walking with a friend and they were approaching us. He passed right by me, and we both said, "Ciao," and kept on walking. Another night, I had been reading in my living room, and when I came back into my room to close my shutters, I saw Beatrice. She was in his apartment standing by the window I had pointed out of and down to my window the first time I was in his apartment. As if being directed for a film, Francesco came out from the kitchen, sauntered over to Beatrice, twirled her around, and they started making out. Then they dropped down and disappeared. I had ducked under my window when I first saw her, and I watched the entire scene play out while holding back a burst of laughter.

I knew that I had finally gotten over him since I was able to laugh as I watched him interact with the woman he really wanted. For a long time, I was so angry at Francesco that whenever I thought about him, my stomach would start hurting. It took me a long time to finally forgive him after God showed me that the reason he had treated me the way he had was because I had allowed him to. I had allowed myself to start liking an older man that I had told myself I wouldn't. How was I supposed to have stopped my heart from falling for him when I had been making every excuse in the book to hang out with him? The reality is that I should've never gotten with him to begin with. I had been at such a low and lonely point that allowing him into my life had ended up doing me more harm than good.

The thing I learned first was to listen to God. When He says, "No," He is telling you that to protect you. After all, God knows everything. In comparison to Him, we know nothing. He knows what's going to happen in the next five minutes; I can only guess what will happen in the next five minutes. To be disobedient to Him is like driving 100 mph with one hand on the steering wheel while blindfolded. Not only is that stupid, but doing that can end up costing you your life. That's exactly what I did—what we all do—when we don't listen to God.

From my experience, I've learned that it's best not to get into a relationship with anyone when you are in a low place emotionally or otherwise. Bad and immature people will use your situation against you. And, you'll make decisions from your pain. Decisions made when you aren't in a good place usually turn out to be disastrous. Eventually, the clouds would've cleared for me, and I would've started to feel more comfortable in Florence and in my own skin. In those moments of despair, they feel like and even seem like they will last forever. They never do. They always get better. I never allowed myself to just take a chance and see if that would truly happen. Instead, I reached out to get my wounds healed by a man who couldn't even handle his own mess. Although he was much older than me, he was very immature. I learned that age truly means nothing in terms of a person's maturity level.

There are also standards that I had for myself that I completely tossed to the side just so I could keep entertaining the company of a man that I would've never looked twice at in my own country. The involvement with him ruined many months of my time in Florence. Not only did I waste months of falling deep into lust with him, I spent even more time leaving him, running back, leaving again, and then having to do the work with God to heal my heart. The good times I did have with him could never make up for all of the bad times I had with him. And for what? Just to say that I had an Italian "friend" and was able to practice the language with him? None of that was worth it.

He did end up holding the mirror up to my face though. Through him, I learned not to keep running back to someone who clearly doesn't want me or someone that I clearly don't even want. Relationships are work, but it's not soul-sucking or draining work: especially if the relationship is healthy and both parties are giving to each other. Unfortunately, my view of love and relationships was so skewed that I believed that I was supposed to chase after love. I also believed that it was okay to use people for my fulfillment. I believed that I could win the attention and full love of someone if I just gave a little more or if I just said the right thing. Even though I didn't truly like him, I still wanted to win him over. In some twisted way, I felt that if I could show him that I was better than the woman he was still in love with, then I would be deemed worthy.

I kept throwing my pearls before swine. Time and time again, they would stomp all over the pearls and then run me over. Bruised and battered, I'd sit up, go dig up the pearls, and then toss them to those men all over again. It's like no matter how beaten down I got, the neurons in my brain didn't fire off enough to tell me that what I was doing was not love. Constantly throwing away my needs, standards, and morals just to say I had someone was a loud signal letting that person know that I didn't love myself and I didn't respect myself. So, if I didn't love myself or respect myself, then why would they?

I blamed my decisions on my past and the fact that I was never taught better. Even though I knew not to do certain things, I still did them and blamed everything and everyone else for my problems. Well, continuing to point the finger at everyone else will never get you to a place where you can finally heal and do better. Yes, he was wrong for putting me through the wringer. I was equally wrong for allowing him to mistreat me.

None of us should ever, ever compromise any of our morals or values to gain anyone's attention, and that includes knowing that your body was not made to catch or keep a man. Trust me. I've tried it, and it has failed every single time. At the age of five, I was molested by a family friend and then exposed to pornography a year later. I knew what sex and masturbation were before I knew how to multiply numbers. I had lust in my heart that I had been feeding since the age of five. I would make out with boys and do heavy petting, but never went past that. I never had to use any type of sex appeal to get a guy's attention. Most guys would just notice me. Once we were "together," I would use my lips and hands to keep them around. I felt comfortable doing those things.

I relied on using my body because I never felt like I was enough. Now I know that who I am, and who you are, *is* enough. That means that if you are doing your best to be the best version of yourself and someone doesn't want you, then that has nothing to do with you. If you want them to love you and see you, and they aren't, that doesn't mean that you should start acting like someone you believe they'll like. Never compromise your standards; be your true self.

You are worth more than being in someone's life just to help them fill a void. If they aren't helping you grow, then don't keep them around. On the flip side, don't just keep someone in your life because they are helping to fill *your* voids. Don't allow yourself to be cheapened, and don't exploit another person's insecurities, but be courteous to others. Have enough integrity to let the person know that they don't fit into your life—even if that means hurting their feelings. It's better to hurt them now than to allow them to be strung along. If someone doesn't see your value, then you don't need to beg them to see it.

Most importantly, God won't give you peace about something He hasn't authorized. Sometimes, we do things on our own, then find that we don't have peace about them, so we try to ask God to give it to us. He's sitting back like, "I never told you to do that in the first place." You may be in complete anxiety about something and asking God to give you peace. The peace may be in you leaving that situation altogether or never stepping into the situation in the first place. God had initially told me not to go into Francesco's apartment. He knew that by doing that, I would open the door to other things and then open it more and more. Once I had finally fallen down the rabbit hole, I had to find a way to stop myself from falling and get back to the door I had initially opened, walk through it, and close it.

God will help you get out of your mess. But, it's better to just avoid the mess in the first place. Once your mess is cleaned up, you can't then look at God and blame Him. You have to look at yourself. You ignored the red flags. You ignored His voice. (I did all of that.) Don't dig yourself into a hole. Don't serve yourself poison and then wonder why you're dying.

There will come a time when you look back on your life and begin to romanticize the bad times. What I mean is that you will start to miss the times you had with someone who treated you badly. You'll make up in your mind that what they did to you wasn't so bad. You'll find yourself wishing that you could be with them again to make things right. I urge you to keep looking forward. You will forget the pain, just don't forget the lesson the pain taught you. Forgive and let go of the bitterness, just don't allow your mind to talk you into going back to a situation that sucked the life out of you. Instead, learn what a real, healthy relationship is, what it feels like, and what it looks like.

I can sit here all day and tell you not to be desperate and tell you to love yourself. You may say, "Well yeah, I don't want to be desperate, and I want to love myself." The best thing I can tell you to do is take some time to figure out what it is that you truly believe about yourself and why. I also advise analyzing your previous relationships and asking yourself how you felt when you were in them. Even though I always felt empty, needy, fearful, and anxious in my relationships, I stayed in them because those were normal feelings for me. In fact, that's how I had always felt around my dad. So, being with men who didn't seem to care about me, ignored my feelings and my boundaries, and made me feel like I wasn't a priority, felt wrong, but it was also normal to me.

My dad also never spoke life over me nor taught me how to interact with men in a healthy and mature way. Then again, my dad wasn't the healthiest person. He was pretty toxic. I learned in a passive way what to expect in relationships based on how he treated me and my mom. There was also no way that I could come out of that environment without bringing those toxic behaviors into my relationships. Deep down, I knew that how I was acting with men was wrong. I knew

I was chasing men in order to fill that empty void inside of me. Instead of bringing those issues to God as I should've, I carried my baggage to men, hoping that they would carry it for me. They ended up using me and making me feel worse than I ever would have, had I just stayed by myself.

Sometimes, being alone is much better than being in a relationship that drains you. I've also been in my share of toxic relationships to know that if you notice the red flags, chances are they are not going to go away if you don't call them out and confront them. Ignoring things and trying to act blissful can also cost you your life; that's not worth it. Jesus already died on the cross for you so that you wouldn't have to get with men who only want to use and abuse you and then lie and call that love.

Love will never drag you through the mud. A loving relationship is meant to add to your life and make you feel refreshed, not anxious and wondering if they're going to leave you. Love is also not sharing a man with another woman. If you want to be loved, I truly understand that. I want you to know that love will one day come from a man—if that is what you desire. However, you first have to allow God to love you and to fill you up, and you have to learn to love and respect yourself. If you go looking for love in other people, they will never be able to give you all that you need. They are some of the icing on top of the cake; they should never be the entire cake.

To get to a place where you can fully love God and love yourself, you will have to go through a season of purging. You'll have to get rid of your limiting and toxic beliefs about yourself, about love, and about God. Then you'll go into a season of healing where you'll have to learn how to be kind to yourself, what real love is, and what God's true character is like.

Today, I finally have a healthier view of myself and of men because I finally listened to God and started doing the work that I needed to do to heal. He wanted me to take marriage and men off of the pedestal I had placed them on. The only perfect man to have ever walked this Earth was Jesus. To think that any man I meet now could save me had caused me to put up with so much unnecessary nonsense. If your relationship is draining you, it's time to get out. Yes, you invested time. Yes, you gave him your body. Yes, to all of those things. Take the loss and move on. You don't want to waste any more of your life watering a seed that will never grow. Once you leave, don't look back, but keep looking forward because God has so much in store for you. He just needs you to take the first step.

Chapter Five

EVERY VICTORY STARTS WITH A MOUNTAIN

"I DON'T THINK I'LL be able to keep going." My breathing was heavy, and my abdomen felt like it was being twisted like a wet towel. I wanted to tumble over, so I sat down on a boulder that was resting in the tall, green grass.

"We can try to meet you on the other side," Courtney said, her voice devoid of emotion and sympathy. A wave of sadness washed over me, and I felt my eyes getting hot. No one seemed to care about me giving up. Did they not care if I joined them or not?

They kept on walking up the hill as I sat on the boulder sulking. I didn't want to get left behind in the middle of the wilderness. I took a deep breath and murmured, "God, I need your help." After my tongue said the word "help," I felt a jolt of energy surge through my body. It was as if I'd just eaten a can of spinach, like Popeye, and I was able to make it to the top of the hill without stopping.

"I'm glad you didn't stay back," Jessica said to me as I collapsed onto a stone bench. The German lady, Anne, who had joined us for the day, was sitting on the stone wall eating an apple.

Jessica had her camera up to her face, pointing it at me. I moved my hand over my eyes. Now was not the time to have a photo shoot.

"Ah, Kio, come on," she begged.

"I just need to catch my breath."

"When you're done, you have to come see the view," Jessica said before walking away.

I raised my eyebrows at her. Where I sat, I could see the water and nothing else. My cramps were more important than any view, plus I wanted to wallow in my despair until they were ready to go back down the mountain. I was waiting for someone to come over and ask me if I was okay when Jessica reappeared and said, "Dude. Seriously."

I let out a quick puff of air and placed my feet on the cobblestones. Courtney was near the edge of the stone wall with her camera raised to her face. The closer I got to her, the more I heard the shutter sound from her camera going off every five seconds. Now standing in the middle of the platform, I turned around to look in the direction I had just come from. I froze.

My eyes started dancing over the view, taking in an image they had never seen before. A deep peace fell over me as I looked out at the expansion of water. The water and the skies were so blue that I couldn't tell where the water ended and the sky began. The homes with coral-colored roofs that settled in with the blue background looked as though they had been strategically placed there by someone. There was water all around me. Even fog was coming up from some areas of the sea. The sea kept going, even though my eyes couldn't behold the extent of their grandeur. I had never seen anything so beautiful in all of my life.

I couldn't look at that and not see the work of an artist. It was like this artist knew exactly what to put there to capture everyone's attention. It was so captivating that Courtney couldn't stop taking pictures, and I just couldn't stop staring. I couldn't tell the sea how beautiful it looked, nor could I thank Courtney or Jessica for putting the sea there. I could only thank God. Even when I see a beautiful person or a beautiful sunset, I know God did that. He makes beauty. He is the greatest creator and artist of all time. In fact, He is the only creator.

God is the only artist that cannot be replicated. His work is original, perfect, and leaves people all over the world speechless. We can make pictures that mimic the work that has already been created. We can use brushstrokes and paint to make a picture of a sunset or a mountain or even an ocean. But, can we make a sunset, a mountain, or an ocean?

He created fish, oceans, and mountains from scratch. He made this entire world from scratch. He made the beautiful, panoramic, Italian scenic views that I had the blessing to see all from scratch. As I was looking at the magnificence around me, all I could say was, "Wow!" That word was the closest expression that could touch the immensity of the greatness my eyes were capturing. Even the "wow" was not good enough. No word was good enough. Not even a picture could do justice to a beauty like that.

We could've stayed up there all day—at least I could've. The sun was getting brighter, so we decided to go explore more of Cefalù before getting on the train back to Palermo. Our trek down the hill spilled over into a trek around the city as we followed Jessica around so she could find *brioche con gelato*. Eventually, we ended up at a gelateria that had the fluffy bread and fresh gelato that Jessica was looking for. I'd never even heard of *brioche con gelato* but decided to try it. After telling the clerk what I wanted, I was staring down at pistachio and hazelnut gelato sandwiched in between sweet bread. To digest our treats, we ended up finding a private beach and hanging out on the sand as the waves washed up on the shore and the sun descended below the sea.

I was just so happy and at peace. When I looked at those amazing landscapes, I realized that beauty like that has a creator. God knows humans so well that He made a bunch of pretty things—oceans, waterfalls, flowers, and birds—for us to admire daily. I mean, He did make us. He would be the one to know what is beautiful to our eyes.

I almost missed out on the opportunity to see such a magnificent image because I wanted to sit, sulk, and cry about having cramps. God had placed that view right in front of me; He delivered it on a silver platter. But, at times, we are too caught up in focusing on the pain that we forget that He wants to bring us peace. Sure, things hurt, and sure, there are lessons to be learned. But, if we continue to focus on the pain, we'll never move past it and be able to experience peace or learn the lesson He is offering us.

Don't get caught up in hiking the mountain, going through all of the muscle aches to get to the top, getting there, and then complaining about how tough the journey was. We forget that we should instead be rejoicing: smiling through the difficult times. Sure, the journey was tough, but look at where it brought you. Don't forget to look around you and appreciate where you are.

SO SIMPLE, YET
SO DELICIOUS

"MMMM ... OH my gosh. Girl, this is so good!" Courtney proclaimed as she sipped her hot chocolate.

I couldn't help but smile.

"How did you find this place?" she asked, smacking her lips.

We were sitting on a terrace, surrounded by students seated at tables with their espressos, croissants, books, and laptops. The air was fresh, with a slight breeze that seemed to blow away the summer heat with each wave.

"A friend ... I mean, someone brought me here. A while ago."

"Oh, a *friend*, huh? Are they *Italian*?" she asked.

"Yeah," I said, looking down at my hot chocolate before taking a sip and saying, "my neighbor."

"Look at you, already making Italian friends."

I liked hanging out with Courtney because she had an easygoing personality. We could spend hours talking about nothing or talking about our fears, desires, God, and any topic that seemed interesting. I remember being in Sicily with her and hanging out on a beach that had pure white sand and clear, light blue water. The weather was so perfect that I wasn't sweating even though the sun was shining on us. Although we were surrounded by beauty, the only thing we could focus on and laugh about was something entirely different.

"The other day I went to Sean Groomis's office to ask him a question, and you know what he told me?" I said, trying to hold back my laughter.

"Oh no. What happened?" She said, leaning in.

"He said that he was out with some Italian professors at dinner, and he was telling everyone a story or something. And then out of nowhere, the man sitting next to him said something like, 'Wow! You have a lot of chest hair.'" Courtney and I started laughing.

"Oh my gosh!" Courtney remarked.

"And then he said the man grabbed one of his chest hairs and pulled it out, like this." I pulled a five-inch imaginary hair out from my chest.

"No way! Ewww. Oh my gosh! He grabbed his chest hair?"

Courtney and I had now rolled over and were laughing while lying on the sand. I did my best to regain my composure.

"I guess he wanted to come out and say 'Hi,'" Courtney said between snickers.

"Buongiorno," I said while using my fingers to mimic chest hair blowing in the wind.

"Oh my gosh, buongiorno! That's what we should name his chest hair!"

The nickname for Sean Groomis's chest hair became "Buongiorno" because it was always peeking out from under his shirt as if it wanted to say "Hi" to everyone.

Not only was Courtney my laughing and conversation partner and travel buddy, she was also my food friend. With her, I was able to try *arancini* (these delicious rice balls that can be filled with cheese, carbonara, or spinach), octopus, pigeon, and our all-time favorite: baked *gnocchi* and cheese. She even snuck into my apartment, along with my friend Brenda, at five in the morning (with the help of my roommate) to cook me French toast on my birthday.

She had been telling me about a sandwich place that she went to when we first got to Florence. She didn't know where it was, but she wanted to take me there. So, after school one day, we went on an adventure to find the sandwich spot.

"Do you at least know what it's called?" I asked Courtney as we made our way down one of the busy streets in Florence.

"I don't know. I know it's off one of these streets. The sandwiches are so good, girl," she said.

It was as if she was being guided by an internal map. When I heard her say, "There it is," I was looking down a dark alley; the perfect place for someone wanting to commit a crime in secret. I followed Courtney into an even darker and tinier room. There were bar stools lined up along the wall and two tiny tables in the middle. At the back wall was a guy our age standing behind a counter. Beyond that, the restaurant didn't even have a kitchen—just an oven and an area where it looked like the bread was made and baked.

"Buongiorno," we all said to one another as we walked in.

"What do you want, girl?" Courtney asked me as she was looking at the menu. There were no more than six items on the menu: lampredotto, tuna, and probably a salami sandwich because … Italy.

"Mmm," I said, studying the menu as I tried to keep myself from being disappointed at the lack of options.

"I want to get the lampredotto sandwich. I've been wanting to try it," she said.

"What is that?"

"Cow stomach."

"Oh," I said, pursing my lips.

"Yeah, girl."

"I think I'll get the tuna sandwich with balsamic and onions," I said.

"Ohhhh, that sounds goooood."

Everything always seemed to sound good to her, even the things that sounded gross to me. We both ordered our sandwiches. Courtney went over to get some napkins. I stood by the counter. The guy opened up a large can of tuna, scooped some out onto the toasted focaccia bread, then laid the onions on top and drizzled it with the vinegar. My sandwich was done in less than two minutes. I looked down at the tuna, onions, and bread. *Why did I order this?* Courtney was now at my side, looking down at my sandwich with a wide grin on her face. I couldn't smile, just stare. Pushing past my imminent disappointment, I took a bite. As I chewed and the items danced over my taste buds, my body lit up.

"Mmm!" I proclaimed.

Courtney looked at me as though I was holding a check for one million dollars. When I finally swallowed, I said, "Oh man, this is delicious," before taking another bite. Courtney got her sandwich. I watched her chew in silence. She vowed to go to other sandwich spots to try their sandwiches until she found one she liked.

From this experience, I learned not to judge a book by its cover. Don't miss out on something just because it isn't packaged the way you think it should be. There are plenty of things (and people) that *look* good but are not good for us. Don't be afraid to inquire. Of course, don't inquire if it means putting yourself at risk in any way.

Chapter Seven

HUMANITY

"WHAT TIME SHOULD we leave here to walk to the bus stop?" I asked Courtney.

"I think we should leave at around 4:15. It shouldn't take us too long to walk there," she said.

My stomach dropped.

"Where is the bus stop anyway?" I asked.

"It's near the train station."

"Maybe we should leave at around 3:45 to give us some time to find the bus stop, just in case we can't find it. I get out of class at 3:30 anyway. We can grab some pizzettas and then walk over."

"Ohh pizzettas. Okay, let's do it. We can leave right after class."

With pizzettas stuffed in brown paper bags, we strolled through the streets in the direction of the train station. The pigeons were flying low. One almost flew into my chest. We were in good spirits, and Courtney had this piece of paper in

99

her hand that I believe was a confirmation of our bus ticket purchases. We arrived at the Santa Maria Novella train station and looked around for a location for the buses and saw some buses parked alongside the station. We went over to a man who was at a stand near the buses.

"Mi scusi. Stiamo cercando per questo l'autobus." (Excuse me. We are looking for this bus.) Courtney handed the paper over to the man. "Lei sa dov'è?" she asked. (Do you know where it is?)

He took the paper, looked it over, and scratched his head.

"Deviamo andare lì," he said, pointing to a building across the street. (You need to go over there.)

"Grazie mille," we said before walking away.

Inside the building were tellers and people standing in a line. We stood there for about five minutes until the lady behind the desk said, "Prego." (Next.)

"Buongiorno. Dov'è questo l'autobus? Va all'aeroporto a Bologna," Courtney asked as she handed the paper to the woman. (Good afternoon. Where is this bus? It goes to the airport in Bologna.)

The lady took the paper. She stared at it, pursed her lips, and tapped her finger on the desk. I watched as the lady's mind was trying to figure out a response for us. She got up from her desk and said, "Un attimo," and walked away. (One second.)

Courtney and I looked at each other.

"Was there an address on there?" I asked. *If there was an address, we probably wouldn't be asking for help right now.* I hoped that Courtney wouldn't answer my dumb question.

"It just has the name of the bus company. I checked online to see where it was, and everything I read said that it was near the station." Courtney's tone was calm and nonjudgmental.

"Allora," the lady said.

She sat back down on her seat. She told us that the bus we were looking for wasn't at this station and that it should be at another location nearby.

"Okay, grazie," Courtney said, sounding hesitant as she took the paper back.

I looked up and saw the clock on the wall. It was now 4:00 p.m. My heart started racing.

"Maybe we can go and look around the corner to see if there's another bus location. Or, we can ask someone," I offered.

Since neither of us had smartphones that had Internet access, we had to rely on the directions from locals and our investigative skills to guide us. Looking around the building proved to be a futile task. The time was getting closer to 4:30 p.m., and no one, not even people working behind a desk, knew where the bus stop was, so we decided to try our luck and find this mysterious location ourselves.

We power walked all around the station, looking down streets to see if we could see any random buses parked that had the company's name we were looking for. We talked to a few more random locals and received some vague directions from them. We even ran down to the end of one of the streets, following someone's directions and still saw nothing. I even took the paper to look at it. Courtney was right that the company's name was on there but nothing else. Who knew that finding a bus would be so difficult?

"It's four twenty," I said, looking at my phone. I clicked my teeth and sighed.

"I don't know, girl. Maybe I can try to get a Wi-Fi signal somewhere." Now Courtney sounded flustered.

"Umm …" I said while clicking my teeth again. My eyes scanned their surroundings. I saw a bald man standing on the sidewalk, talking and gesticulating to one of his friends. I walked right up to him. I smiled, showing my teeth, and waved to get his attention. He was still talking, but he looked at me.

"Buongiorno," I said, still waving.

"Ah, ciao, buongiorno, Signorina," he greeted me.

"Mi puoi aiutare?" I asked. (May you please help me?)

"Dipende," he said, looking at his friend. (It depends.)

We all laughed.

"Sto cercando per un'autobus che va in Bologna. Non lo so dov'è e parte fra dieci minuti. Lo sai dov'è?" I asked, doing my best to form a coherent sentence. (May you please help me? I am looking for a bus that goes to Bologna. I don't know where it is, and it leaves in ten minutes. Do you know where it is?)

He glanced down at the paper and without hesitation said, "Sì! Vai sempre dritto. Sempre, sempre dritto. Non vai alla destra o la sinistra. Sempre dritto. Poi alle fine della strada, vedrai l'autobus." (Yes, go straight. Stay straight. Don't go to the right or to the left. Then, at the end of the street, you'll see the bus.)

As he spoke, his arms were waving in the air. He kept pointing straight down the street with his arm.

"Grazie mille!" I said and turned to Courtney. "He said it's at the end of the street."

"We just came from there," she said.

"Yeah, I know. But it won't hurt to check again. If we miss it, we'll have to catch the train or something. It's worth a try."

"You're right," she said.

I turned away and ran down the street. Courtney was right beside me as we dodged pedestrians. My backpack pounded against my back. We ran in the street, making sure to look out for cars. I slowed down and stopped at the end of the street. I was out of breath. I looked around and scoffed.

"I don't see anything." Courtney sighed.

My heart was pounding so hard, and I could barely breathe. I took a moment to think back to the encounter with the man. In my mind, I saw his hand making a gesture in the air, as if making a covering with his hands. *Why did he say that it was straight?* I looked to my left and saw an underpass. Cars were speeding down the road; some were going east while the others were going west. I ran in the direction of the underpass. As I was running to go under the underpass, I looked across the busy street and saw a hot pink bus parked on a small side street off the main road.

"Oh my gosh! The bus is over there," I yelled over at Courtney while pointing across the street.

"No way!" She was now running towards me, panting.

"How are we going to get over there?" I asked, trying to catch my breath.

She was now by my side. "We have to run across the street. There's no time to go all the way to the end and come back down," Courtney said.

I didn't have time to object about how scared I felt about crossing one of the busiest streets I'd seen in Florence. People already drove crazy, and I wasn't ready to end my life just to catch a bus. As I was debating with myself, Courtney was looking both ways and stepping out onto the street. I had no choice but to follow her. There was silence: no oncoming cars sneaking around the bend. We took the opportunity and ran across the first lane. We stopped in a middle lane as cars sped past us. Our feet hit the pavement as soon as the next lane was clear, and we didn't stop until we got to the bus and showed the man the paper. There wasn't any time to care about everyone staring at us as we made our way to our seats. We had no sooner sat down than I felt the rumble of the engine. All I could do was pant and remove some of my layers of clothing.

"Oh my gosh." I laughed as I fanned myself with my hand.

"We actually made it. That was crazy," Courtney said, panting as well.

When the bus dropped us off at the Bologna airport, we got on our plane. Disembarking from the plane, we got on a bus that dropped us off at the center of the town.

"Let's see where we're going," said Courtney, and she pulled out the printed directions of the route from the bus station to the hostel. We both looked up to see where we were in relation to the map. At the same time, a man walking by was looking back at us. Our gazes met his, so he stopped, walked towards us, and asked, "Do you need help?"

He held his hand up at us as to say, "Don't be afraid," as he approached us. I heard a slight Polish accent when he spoke. Courtney and I looked at each other.

"Uh yeah." Courtney chuckled. "We're looking for Kraków Hostel. It looks like it's in the middle of the square."

"Yes, yes," he said, gazing down at the paper. "If you just walk this way, you will enter the square. It is very large. You can just walk straight, and you will arrive at the hostel. There will be no problem finding it."

"Great! Thank you!" I said.

"Thank you," Courtney said.

"Where are you from?" he asked, looking at us.

"Oh, we're American," Courtney said.

"American? What brings you to Poland? It is so far from America."

"We're actually studying in Italy right now. But we came here to go to Auschwitz," I said.

"You are students," he said, smiling at us. "Welcome to Poland. I hope you enjoy. Good luck."

"Thanks!" we said to him as he walked away.

"Wow, people here are so nice," I said as Courtney and I walked toward our hostel.

"Seriously," she replied.

...

I was wearing a grey wool sweater over an undershirt and stockings underneath my leggings. My wool socks were shoved into my brown ankle boots. My wool coat and wool scarf sealed everything in. I looked up at Courtney to see that her head was down, looking at her camera. I gazed out the window and saw grey covering the landscape outside. Everything looked cold. The vibrant green and blue skies that I saw in Florence were now replaced by grey hues, making the fields and sky look dull. I saw people getting on and getting off of the train. I wasn't sure of when we were meant to disembark. I wondered if Courtney knew. I had already asked her a few questions about the name of the stop and didn't want to bother her again. I was nervous about missing the stop and I decided to inquire once more.

"Do you know which stop we get off at?"

She looked up. "It's okay, girl. We won't miss it. We have to be on here for three hours."

"Oh, three hours? Okay. I see." I felt more at ease.

Our goal was to make it to the camp by 1:00 p.m. so that we could go on a walking tour with a tour guide. We left Kraków a little bit before 10:00 a.m., and when the train finally arrived in Auschwitz, it was close to 1:00. Getting off of the train and walking through the town was a bit of a blur to me. The town was desolate. Cars weren't loud, and they weren't roaring by like they did in Florence. There were people out, yet it wasn't lively. No one was having an intense conversation. I didn't see kids running around and playing either. This might have been because of the time of year. I felt my bones clench from the chill in the air. I held on to my body to help generate some heat. My toes were numb, and I felt like I was breathing in dry ice.

The feeling didn't go away, not even when we arrived at the camp. At the entrance of the gate, written in large steel letters was the phrase "Arbeit macht frei." (Work sets you free.) When we went to buy our tickets, we asked if there was a tour available. We had arrived five minutes too late because the last tour of the day had already left, and they were already walking around the grounds.

Before going to visit the camp, I had a vision of some things that I would do while I was there. On the list of things to do was go on the tour, but that didn't happen. I had also seen myself in deep thought as I scribbled words into my leather-bound journal. I didn't even bring my journal, so that couldn't happen either. I had also envisioned Courtney and I having a deep conversation about everything we had witnessed.

As Courtney and I wandered around the premises, the only thing I heard was silence, except for our feet making crunching sounds as they moved across the dirt path. Seeing the piles of hair that belonged to some Jewish women inside of a glass container left me speechless. I even stood in an area where they would line the prisoners up against the wall and gun them down. The gas chambers looked like a large brick oven set in the middle of a concrete room. I got scared as I walked through the oven, thinking that the gas would turn on and suffocate me with its fumes. I walked in, glanced around, and scurried out. Once I made it back outside, I gasped for air. I hadn't realized that I was holding my breath.

It's freezing out here. No amount of walking or ducking into some of the buildings helped me to generate enough body heat. My mind kept bringing up images of the naked prisoners being marched in a line outside. I saw them standing on the ground shivering: their bodies devoid of any fat to insulate them. I was dressed in the warmest clothes I owned, and I was still freezing. I could only imagine how the prisoners felt.

When our emotions became overwhelmed with grief and our bodies became numb from the coldness, we shuffled back through the steel gates and dragged ourselves to the station. I couldn't think of anything to say on the train back to Kraków, and neither could Courtney. I still needed to take everything in that I had witnessed.

…

Going to the death camp was one of the most eye-opening and depressing experiences of my life. To go and see places where history took place is not about going back and trying to relive a moment, or even trying to open up to experiencing what people went through during those times. We can never be put in the position that the people taken to the death camp were put in. No number of reenactments or focused meditations will give us that type of experience. We can, however, learn from history so that we do not repeat such heinous acts.

To know that another human had an evil thought and then carried out that thought not only scared me, but it bothered me to no end. Perhaps it bothered me because I realized that we all have the same nature, and we all have the capacity to do evil. Everyone will not act on the evil thoughts they have, but I'm pretty sure all of us have had evil thoughts before.

It also hit me that the reason it was easy for the Nazis to treat the Jews so horribly was because they didn't even see them as humans. This is so heartbreaking. Everyone around me is my equal. We are all equals because we are all equally human. No one is more or less human because they have more or less melanin, straighter hair, or a different eye color. We are all made in the image of God, and we need to treat everyone with respect.

Chapter Eight
GET YOUR GREEK ON

THE TELEVISION IS set to Food Network. The camera pans over the water and zooms in on a balcony where a lady named Giada is with another woman. The woman lays a thin pastry into a baking dish, sprinkles it with a ground-up mixture of nuts and spices, and continues the layering process. When the last piece of pastry is laid on top, she soaks the pastry with what she says is honey and then sticks black cloves onto the top of the pastry. They say that they are in "Santorini" and call what they just made "baklava."

My twelve-year-old eyes are so captivated by what they see. I've never heard of baklava or Santorini, and all I know is that I want to eat baklava and go to Santorini. I take out my journal, and with a red pen and sloppy writing, I write, "I'm going to Santorini to eat baklava."

Ten years later, I woke up on the island of my dreams. I decided to wear my cream and colorful scarf because I wanted to be prettier, more presentable, and more lively than the black I kept wearing. *No, I am in Santorini and need a change of scenery on my body.*

I was up and dressed before Courtney and Reese, and since we had not planned a set time to do anything, decided that I would have some quiet time with God. Perhaps being on vacation is a free pass for automatically being at peace, but I wasn't feelin' it, so I prayed. I spent some time asking God for protection over myself and my friends and prayed that this day would go smoothly and that we would find awesome things to do.

With prayer time over and with the promise of catching the bus into Fira town to buy fresh fruit, my friends and I left our place to wait around for the bus to arrive. Once at the bus stop, all of us looked skeptically at one another, trying to find out what time the bus came and how much it would cost based off of each other's expressions.

"George never told us how much a bus ticket costs," remarked Reese.

"Yeah, but I'm sure we can just buy it on the bus," I replied, hoping that what I was saying was true.

The next surge of words came from Reese as she looked across the street.

"Can we run over there so I can look for an iPhone charger?" she asked.

"Sure," Courtney and I said.

We walked across the street and into the store where she bought an iPhone charger, then we headed back across the semi-crowded street to the bus stop.

Perhaps I was lost in my own thoughts because something caused me to walk ahead of my friends. Double-checking the street, I looked to my left and saw that no cars were coming and then over to my right and saw clarity. I stepped into the street. I looked to my left again and I froze. The only thing I could do was freeze. I could not think of any other way to conduct myself. *Oh, crap.* My chest tightened and I gasped. I saw a fat man on a motorbike coming right at me. He was swerving.

The impact forced out all of the air inside of my body. I let out a half whimper-half shriek. I felt something lift me up and thrust me onto the front of the bike. My hands searched to grab on to a solid foundation. We rode together for about five feet before the bike screeched to a complete stop.

Still frozen, I looked with wide eyes into the eyes of this man. He glared at me with wider eyes and grabbed me with both of his hands and thrusted me back onto solid ground. I stood there, staring at him. My friends were by my side asking if I was okay. His entire face was red, and scrunched up, and his mouth was wide open. He raised his hand in the air as if he were about to slap me across the face.

My body snapped back to reality. *Hitting me after hitting me? What?*

With his hand hovering in the air, he paused for a second, lowered his hand, looked me in the eyes and yelled, "Stupid!"

"No!" I screamed.

He rambled words off in Greek, probably cursing me, then drove off into paradise.

"Thank you, God. Thank you, Jesus! Oh my gosh," was all I kept saying.

The concern of my friends was on full blast as they tried their best to console me and ask me if I was okay. I wasn't lying when I said that I was fine because I was. I only suffered trauma on my right hand, where a previous scar received a new wound from the impact. Other than a little bit of blood and pain, I was fine. I was so physically untouched by the incident that my white shirt was still as clean as it had been when I had put it on that morning. I told my friends that I was okay, and while walking away from them, I said, "I just need a minute."

As soon as I sat down on the bench, I started weeping. I was crying tears of joy because I was alive, and I was weeping tears of shock and guilt because I had just been in an accident. Maybe some tears of, *What the eff, Kio! Pay more attention!* were mixed in there too.

I was thankful for my friends for being so attentive and actually showing concern for me. Even the simplest act of asking me if I was okay was enough. The biggest scar I received was not from getting hit, it was from seeing that man raise his hand at me. That hurt me more than anything because that was the biggest symbol of disrespect.

"Had he slapped you, I would've lost it," proclaimed Reese as we walked away from the scene of the accident.

We rented a car so that it would be easier for us to explore the island. Driving around in search of a lighthouse, spending time in Fira town, getting lost as we tried to find a beach, then being stopped by a tribe of goats were our adventures for the day. Being able to drive around the island was nice because I was able to see the other parts of Santorini that are not featured on any postcards. After failing to find one of our destinations, we pulled off to the side of a random road to take a picture of the scenery. We then ended up following

Courtney as she led us on a hike down a mountain to a red pebble beach. Even though I was fully clothed, I couldn't help but dip my legs, which were exposed by rolling up my jeans, into the water, then lie on the damp pebbles as the water washed up underneath me. That was a great feeling.

...

The sun was set to rise at 6:30 a.m. Thanks to George— the owner of our bed and breakfast—we were awakened at 6:00 a.m. We hopped in the car and parked it on a black sand beach. I saw this orange circle rise up from the ocean as its presence painted the sky with streaks of oranges and golds and ribbons of purples and blues. It was a beautiful sight. And yet, beauty without impression was the theme for my entire stay in Santorini. Sights were beautiful—picturesque even. But nothing, not one image, made me step back and grab on to something to keep me from falling over in awe.

Tired from our early morning rising, my friends and I chose to lay around for a bit, and after returning the car, ventured into Fira town. We were able to walk there within fifteen minutes, and on the way, ran into a dog that my friends so graciously named Pooka. This day marked the second day we were visiting this town, mainly because it was so conveniently located and had everything we needed, including entertainment.

We made our way down a road to the old port. As we walked, we had to take careful steps on the slippery cobblestones while dodging donkey droppings and avoiding donkeys that passed by on our left and right. At one point, we were stuck in traffic and could not move until the donkeys and humans were able to move along in harmony. Courtney and I were stopped right next to the back of a donkey. I watched as the donkey's butthole opened, vibrated, and let out a long winded sound before closing. I immediately held on to my breath for dear life and frantically looked around for a place to escape so that I could breathe. When I looked to my right, Courtney was staring at me with a horrified yet amused expression. Seeing her face made me snicker, which was a big mistake, so I turned away from her. She continued giggling beside me as my lungs were begging me to open my mouth so they could get some air. Try as I might, I couldn't hold my breath any longer and finally burst out into laughter with Courtney.

I didn't want to hurt the donkey's feelings by laughing, and I hoped he understood that I was only laughing at the image of his butthole passing gas, not at him. After all, it wasn't his fault that he wasn't able to fart in private.

The traffic finally started moving and we were able to find fresh air and rocks to rest upon down at the port. As my friends rested their feet in the icy Grecian water, music flowed into my ears through my earphones as I danced behind them. When my desire to dance faded, I joined my friends on the rocks so that we could discuss what we wanted to cook for dinner Friday night before leaving. That conversation did nothing in terms of helping us decide what to cook. Instead, it made our stomachs yearn to be filled with food. We took the cable car back into the center and searched for a restaurant with a view.

We were in the perfect position to watch the sunset as we ate our lunch/late dinner of dolmades, tzatziki sauce and pita bread, moussaka, tomato balls, and fried calamari. The clouds did their job of concealing the element that would have added atmosphere to our meal. Nevertheless, we enjoyed our food, and once again, ate more than our stomachs could handle.

"Wow, I am so full. That was good," remarked Courtney, satisfied with our dinner, which reminded her of tapas from Barcelona. Dessert sounded like a good idea at the beginning but became the worst thought ever once we had finished eating. Instead of trying to force solid sugars into our bodies, we ordered liquid sugars in the form of two Sprites and a Coke. To work off our food, we tried on a bunch of different scarves in a shop that we had previously visited hours before. Courtney and Reese both walked away with scarves that brought color to their countenances and their wardrobes. They were glowing.

Courtney and Reese beamed with joy and so did the city of Fira. As the sun disappeared and darkness fell over the town, I was reminded of a word Courtney had used to describe Athens. She had called it the "glistening" city. At night, when the sun was gone and the lights streamed from the windows of the buildings, the city glistened. Just as stars twinkle in the sky, so twinkles the city of Fira in the night. Unfortunately, nightfall also brought with it the cold wind and air, forcing us out of the city and back to the comfort and warmth of our room so that we could rest for the next day.

…

"Good afternoon. Does this café have baklava?" I asked the adorable waiter at a café in Oia (the city you see when you see images of Santorini) that I had randomly decided to walk into.

"Yes, of course, love. Would you like to eat it here or to take it away?" he asked.

After a few minutes' pause to look at my friends, I finally said, "Here is fine."

"Okay, right this way, love."

The day had finally come for me to enjoy the reason I had come to Santorini. As we seated ourselves at a table that had the perfect view of the ocean, the blinding white buildings, and the sloping mountains, I couldn't help but shift with excitement in my seat as I awaited the arrival of my heart's desire.

"Would you like menus to search for drinks to go with your food?" asked the adorable waiter.

"Yes, please!"

"Okay, love."

Ten minutes later, my baklava, Reese's dessert, and our teas were set out in front of us.

"Try some," I said to Courtney, offering her some of the fresh baklava that had just been served to me.

"No, *nooo*. You've been waiting for this. You go first."

"Kerrrr," proclaimed the top layer of baklava as I held it down with my fork and cut into it with my knife. That sound was not only music to my ears, it was also confirmation that I had found the baklava that I was searching for. The crunchiness was the first and basically the only characteristic that I knew I wanted the baklava to have since I was not sure of how it should have tasted. The first piece touched my tongue and I began to chew and taste. Jackpot! That baklava tasted good enough for me to look with wide eyes first at Courtney, then at Reese as contentment filtered throughout my body.

"*Please*, have some," I said, encouraging Reese and Courtney to enjoy with me. Reese was also enjoying her dessert but encouraged us to eat as much as we desired. My baklava and I were in good company with a tea known as The Little Prince, which added the perfect amount of light floral goodness to the experience.

Satisfied, we left that magical café and continued exploring more of Oia. Reese's heart was set on getting a fish pedicure. Our wandering brought us to a place that offered her ten minutes for €10 to have fish suck on her toes. They swarmed like leeches going after their prey as soon as she lowered her feet into the water, and when I saw them swarm, my immediate reaction was, "Eww!"

"It feels like tiny bubbles," Reese said, giggling.

"Ewwww," I groaned.

The even nastier part was when she lifted her feet. The fish, still holding on, did not drop off until they were deprived of oxygen and were forced to let go and dive back into the water. After the fish-feeding frenzy, we found a windmill, had a mini photo shoot, and found a place with a view, where we sat and talked as we waited for our dinner reservation at seven o'clock.

At seven o'clock, we were seated at a table with the perfect view of the sunset. Even though our desire for eating at this restaurant was to watch the sunset while we ate, I was hoping to skip the view and eat inside because I was freezing. The wind was strong and the air was chilly, but we were determined to eat lamb, pasta, and fish as we watched the sunset. However, as fate, or this restaurant, would have it, we did not get our food until after the sun went down. When the sun left, so did everyone else who was at the restaurant. The atmosphere went from chaotic to serene. Care must have been taken in preparing our food because it was completely worth the wait. My lamb was perfectly tender and did not have an overwhelming flavor. The rosemary sauce was a great complement as was the red cabbage and mashed potatoes over eggplant side dish.

Courtney ate grilled fish, while Reese enjoyed her beef, tomato, and pesto pasta. And of course, we shared our meals with one another until we could not eat any more. By the time we were done, we were annoyed because we were so cold. This one man who was having a romantic dinner with his girlfriend could not help but keep his attention on us instead of his date. As he watched us pay for the bill and get up from the table, he directed his remark of, "You must be freezing," towards Courtney, to which she replied, "Yeah, no kidding."

...

We spent the remainder of our time in Santorini eating, walking, and driving around. On Friday, our last day, we found a black pebble beach and made friends with two Greek guys. One of them liked the style of my hair so much that he wanted me to do his like mine. So, there I was, on the beach, flat twisting a Greek guy's hair.

Courtney, Reese, and I made dinner and ate together before they left at midnight to start their journey back to Florence. Their itinerary required them to catch the ferry from Santorini back to Athens. From there, they would take a train ride to Thessaloniki, then get on a flight to Pisa and catch a bus from Pisa to Florence. My itinerary, on the other hand, was catching a flight from Santorini at 7 a.m. to Rome and then taking a train from there to Florence. George so graciously drove them to the port, and then he came to my room at five o'clock as he had promised. As we drove in dead silence to the airport, I looked out the window and up at the sky. The sky was so dark, and placed on the black background was this thin curve of cream. The moon was the thinnest I had ever seen it. It was so beautiful and such a perfect sight to end my time in the place that I had always dreamed of visiting.

My time spent in Greece was by far the most relaxing and peaceful vacation I've ever had. Although most of what I experienced didn't fit my "dream," I learned that life is rarely so neat. Instead of making up in my mind about how I think an experience is supposed to go, I learned to go with the flow and allow things to unravel as they should. Life doesn't need me to try and control it, it just needs me to live it. I truly never thought that my twelve-year-old pipe dream of going to Santorini to eat baklava would come true, yet it did. It wasn't by way of me forcing it to happen. It was me putting it out into the universe and not even questioning if it would happen or not. I knew that was what I wanted, so that's what had to happen, right?

Sure, my time on the island was also met with a bit of resistance. There are obstacles that we face in order to get to our destination. In order for our dreams to come true, we have to jump over our hurdles. Did I need to get hit by a motorcycle? Probably not, but that's a part of my story. That made my time in Santorini even sweeter because I learned to appreciate life even more.

Chapter Nine
THE SWEETNESS OF BEING ALONE

EING IN FLORENCE was like living in a romance novel. At night, the town lit up with yellow lights that seemed to set the mood over the entire city. The sound of accordions flowed through the streets. Couples danced in my favorite piazza as others walked by them; no one was bothered by what the other was doing. Some nights after dinner, I would journal under the loggia in Piazza della Signoria. Or, I would simply walk anywhere, allowing my feet to carry me where they pleased. There was no rush, no time limit to be met. I could just *be* and exist. On some weekends, I would wake up early enough to be one of the first people at Sant'Ambrogio Market. I searched for a golden apple, grapes, pesto, bread, prosciutto, and pistachios. I'd chat with some of the vendors and carry my bounty to one of the bus stops. The bus would drop me off near Palazzo Pitti where I would walk behind the palace and go into Boboli Gardens. I'd spread out on the grass, unpack my food and my journal, and relax. I started taking my time and enjoying the still, almost boring moments. I got a scoop of gelato and ate it as I people watched. Not every moment had to have excitement packed into it. Oftentimes, being quiet and being alone brought the greatest enjoyment.

One day, I mustered up the courage to take a solo day trip to a city called Lucca so that I could ride a bike. I had almost talked myself out of going because I didn't want to go alone. But, I was feeling like I needed a soul revival. I had gone to a soccer game; been on the news; traveled to Spain, Morocco, and Poland; and had explored much of Italy and most of Florence. Life was now normal and had become routine. Nothing exciting was happening anymore. So, to revive my soul, the only thing that made sense was to ride a bike in Lucca.

Lucca is a city known for still having intact city walls. It is possible to walk on these walls, run on these walls, and even bike on these walls. Trees, grass, peace, and harmony are in abundance on top of the walls. I arrived in Lucca and walked aimlessly until I saw the city walls, and then I strolled around them for some time. The more tired my feet grew, the more anxious I became to hop on a bike. I went on a mission, found a shop, and rented a bike for the hour. My heart leaped for joy once I started peddling and picking up speed. Either my smile was irresistible or there was a halo of light around me because everyone was staring at me as if they had never seen a girl on a bike before. After riding on the walls, I explored the center of the city and rode down any street that looked interesting. I only desired to return the bike because the seat was starting to make my butt go numb.

Exploring the city on foot brought me to a bookstore, where I purchased a cookbook, and then to a jewelry stand where I met Roberta and Giovanni. Our forty-minute encounter involved me focusing on what I thought they were saying, then figuring out a proper way to respond. At the end of our conversation, Giovanni gave me a ring: the exact ring I had been eyeing. At the end of my day trip, I felt so happy. I was glad that I hadn't let my fear of being alone keep me from having a good time.

I had a fear that I would somehow die of boredom if I was alone for too long. I also felt that I always needed to have someone around to entertain me because I was incapable of entertaining myself. Sure, some experiences are best enjoyed with friends. But, constantly relying on other people to entertain you could mean that you're trying to run from yourself. At least, that's what I was doing. Whatever I ran from never went away. It just chased after me until I turned around and confronted it. I had to learn how to like myself in order to become comfortable being alone. I did this by taking myself out to get gelato or going to see a movie alone. Sometimes, I'd even go to a café alone and just journal. Yes, it was awkward. Yes, I wished someone was there with me. But, as time went on, I began to feel more comfortable with myself and in my own skin.

Chapter Ten
NEVER FORGET
WHO YOU ARE

ONE OF MY favorite movies growing up was *The Parent Trap*. I watched that movie so much that I memorized just about every line. Even though I knew the scenes from front to back, there was always one that captivated my attention. It's the scene after Annie and Hallie switch places at summer camp. Annie, who is actually Hallie, gets picked up from the airport by her butler, Martin, and is being driven home. Since this is Hallie's first time in London, she sticks her head out of the car window and gawks at the images surrounding her. The people were dressed so elegantly, the black cabs looked like toy cars, and even the buildings were ornately designed. Seeing that movie gave me the desire to go to London.

Years later, I was on a plane going from Florence to London for the weekend. When I got off the plane, this

Black guy with a British accent approached me and asked me where I was from.

"I'm from California," I said.

"I like the accent," he said before power walking away.

"Wait, but I like *your* accent," I wanted to say after him. It hadn't really occurred to me until that moment that I actually had an accent too.

My itinerary for the weekend was to meet up and hang out as much as possible with Courtney and Lisa. I ended up staying at my friend Monica's dorm room in Surbiton—a twenty-minute train ride out of London—while Courtney and Lisa stayed at a hostel somewhere.

The first day, I was set to meet up with Courtney and Lisa at Buckingham Palace at 10:00 a.m. Monica told me to take the train to Waterloo Station and walk across the bridge so that I could see the London Eye, the River Thames, then the Palace of Westminster.

I ended up arriving at Waterloo Station at 9:42 a.m. with Buckingham Palace a good thirty-minute walk from where I was. I knew it was a lost cause trying to rush over there to meet up with my friends. I figured that they would get there at 10:00, not see me, and leave. I strolled through a beautiful garden, took pictures, and saw so many of the black cabs and red phone booths that I wanted to swoon.

I finally meandered up to Buckingham Palace and I saw things I was not expecting to see. There were people—lots of people. I was taking my time walking around while looking for familiar faces. At one point, I asked God what to do because I didn't know where I was going. *Keep walking.* My eyes lit up and I saw two familiar faces.

"Courtney! Lisa!" I proclaimed.

We shared a bunch of laughter and then walked to get high tea. Twenty pounds later and pretty full, we spent the next couple of hours exploring. We went to Primark, walked around trying to find a bookstore, went to a view spot to see the city, then walked for days (seemingly) to go to a place called Ye Olde Cheshire Cheese. Monica had recommended we get fish and chips there because a scene from a Harry Potter movie had been shot at that place.

...

The next day, I got lost trying to find Courtney and Lisa at a breakfast spot and had to get help from a random Brazilian lady. In her high heels, she grabbed my hand and ran with me down the street until she got me to my destination. After eating, we decided to go our separate ways since all of us wanted to do something different. Lisa was taking a bus to Brighton, or some town, and Courtney wanted to go on a Harry Potter Studio Tour. I just wanted to explore as much of London as possible, even thinking I might try to find *The Parent Trap* house.

I took out my tourist map and saw the British Museum on there and headed that way. I kept turning down the wrong street and ending up in the same location. I tried following signs that read "British Museum" with arrows pointing straight. I kept passing the building. I didn't know what the building was supposed to look like. I finally made it inside. I was so happy and flustered that I drew the attention of the security guard manning the door. We ended up chatting for a bit until I told him that I wanted to go check out the museum.

"If we meet again, it is meant to be," he said as I was walking away.

Whatever. I glared at the ring on his finger.

I strolled inside. There were people all around me gawking at tribal masks that were displayed in glass containers. Off in another room were displays of more masks. I saw a large sign that read "AFRICA." Out of nowhere, I was hit with an overwhelming feeling that I needed to see *The Lion King.* Without even looking at any other exhibits, I ran out and went back to the desk where I had been talking to the security guard.

"I need to see *The Lion King*!" I proclaimed, pretty much hyperventilating at this point.

"Oh, right. Yes, of course," the security guard stammered. He looked at me and then looked around. He probably thought someone had chased me out of the room.

"Where is it? Can you help me get there?" I asked.

As if the main security guard had called for backup, another security guard came from behind a door that was behind the desk. Seeing him, I grabbed my map from my backpack and spread it out onto the counter. He smoothed the map out, and I watched as his finger traced a trail from the British Museum to the Lyceum Theatre.

"Can you remember the directions?" he asked.

"Yes! I think I got it. Thank you so much for the help!" I said and ran off.

Knowing my sense of direction, I was surprised I made it there with no problem. One hundred and sixty pounds later,

I had my ticket to see *The Lion King* at a West End theater at 7:30 that evening. It was about two in the afternoon, so to pass the time, I went down to Brick Lane where I found a Starbucks to sit down, get some food, catch my breath, and contact Courtney.

Once I felt calm and knew Courtney was also okay, I exited the Starbucks just as the sky decided to spit out some hail and rain onto everyone below. Thankfully, my umbrella kept me dry as I ventured to an indoor market where I met a man from Athens and purchased two dainty silver rings. Feeling anxious about missing the show, I made my way back to the theater and arrived there entirely too early.

I tried to nap while waiting in my seat for the show to start. Finally, all the lights turned off and everyone made their way onto the stage and started singing. I had to fight myself to stay awake. My favorite part of the play was the part where Simba followed Rafiki through caves and cramped spaces and ended up at a river. He looked into the water and saw his likeness. He looked harder and his likeness morphed into the face of his father, Mufasa. He heard his father's voice call his name.

"Simba, you have forgotten me," Mufasa's spirit said.

"No, how could I?"

"You have forgotten who you are and so have forgotten me … remember who you are. Remember who you are," Mufasa said as his spirit disappeared.

"No, please, don't leave me. Father, don't leave me."

"Never forget who you are."

"Father, why won't you speak to me?" Simba asked.

"I've always been here," Mufasa replied.

Even though I was half asleep and wanting to be back on that blow-up mattress in Monica's dorm, that really spoke to my heart.

I also loved the part where Rafiki hit Simba on the head with his stick, and reacting to the pain, Simba proclaimed, "Ouch! That hurt."

Rafiki came back with, "But it was in the past."

"But it still hurts," Simba said, rubbing his head.

"Oh, yes. The past can hurt. But the way I see it, you can either run from it, or, learn from it," Rafiki said.

…

I hadn't spent too much of my time dreaming about seeing *The Lion King* in London. I can't even remember how I knew *The Lion King* would be in London the same weekend I was there. I just remember having a desire to see the play, never realizing that it would take place in a foreign country. Everything seemed to fall into place that day. It was like God was ordering my steps.

The scene with Mufasa and Simba was the one that captivated my attention more than any other part of the play. Mainly because I literally felt like God was speaking directly to me in that moment. God was beckoning me to remember, like Mufasa was reminding Simba, who I am. I believe that we are all placed on this Earth for a reason. Sometimes we try and do what is comfortable but isn't truly "us." Running from yourself or your past will never work out. It will keep coming back up until you deal with it, and then you will be able to move on to do more. Don't run, confront. Stand in who you are. After all, God made you. So, if He made you who you are, and you don't know how to stand in all of that, ask Him how. Ask Him to give you the strength every day to be who He called you to be, not who the world wants you to be.

Unfortunately, I had made a habit of ignoring God's voice. But I've learned that when I listen to God, things in my life fall into place. I believe God speaks to us through the Bible, through people, and by speaking to us internally—some call it "intuition." There's even a story in the Bible where God made a donkey speak to relay a message to someone. God can use any avenue to get your attention because He's God, and He isn't limited by time, space, or matter. It's that feeling you get when you know that you should or shouldn't do something. Or it might be a case where everything looks great, but deep down you feel that something just isn't right. That's God.

I usually know when God is speaking to me because the feeling I get from "hearing" his voice either brings me peace or it makes me feel convicted. His voice is gentle and kind and never harsh or abrasive. He will never make you feel guilty. He will correct you when you're wrong. The way you know you've been corrected is if you did something and you just don't feel right about it. That is God's spirit convicting your spirit. Know that God speaks to you because He wants to lead you, and He wants to help you because He loves you.

Chapter Eleven

BABY STEPS

"I SOUND LIKE A five-year-old," I heard my classmate Ethan say as I walked into the classroom and put my backpack on my desk.

"Buongiorno," my professor Matteo said to me.

"Ciao, buongiorno," I stammered, looking over at Ethan to see him frowning and looking as though his puppy had run away.

"If you never make a mistake, how will you learn how to speak?" Matteo asked, now looking at Ethan. I sat down slowly into my seat, doing my best to make as little noise as possible.

"It's just so embarrassing. I can speak well in English. In Italian, I sound like a five-year-old when I'm an adult," Ethan said, pouting.

"If a baby never falls down, how will he learn to walk?" Matteo asked, crossing his arms and leaning against his desk.

A light bulb seemed to go off in Ethan's head because he perked up and said, "That's true."

"If you never make a mistake, you can never learn. The baby, he falls down. He wants to walk, but he falls. When he falls to the ground, he gets up, and then he will try again. But if he stays to the ground when he falls, how can he learn to walk? He must keep trying," Matteo said.

I felt the urge to applaud.

Ethan nodded, which prompted Matteo to continue, "It is similar to me when I had to learn English. My speech was not so elegant. I made many mistakes. With many mistakes, my English became better. This will be the case for you. It is okay to sound like a five-year-old when you are learning. With time, the more you make a mistake, your Italian will improve. Okay?"

"Thanks, you're right," Ethan said.

…

I'm not sure what it is about me where I'll hear a conversation between two people—that has nothing to do with me—but as I listen, I end up getting a lesson from their conversation. I remember so vividly how defeated Ethan looked. He was the one who was too shy to read in Italian out loud in class. He hated the way he sounded and hated how he would always mess up on words. So, he stopped trying. I think he was waiting for others to laugh at him because he had already laughed at himself. Honestly, we were all in the same boat. No one was sitting there critiquing each other. We would just do our best to pronounce the words so that our teacher wouldn't have to correct us. I never remember trying to read well, just to earn cool points from my classmates.

Learning a foreign language truly helped me see in real time how consistent steps in any direction build on each other. We started learning the alphabet, numbers, pronouns, and then how to form sentences. At the beginning of my time in Florence, my vocabulary hadn't been developed enough to know what people around me were saying. I would hear, "vieniquavogliodirtiunacosa." No word was distinguishable to me. As time went on, the gibberish became, "vieni qua, voglio dirti una cosa." (Come here. I want to tell you something.) My ears were still the same. It was just that my knowledge for the language had increased, so I was able to understand better.

Initially, a foreign language is going to sound, well, *foreign* to you when you speak it. That's normal. You will sound ridiculous because your tongue is not used to forming these new words, making these new sounds, and rolling the *r*'s. Not only is it a task for your brain, it's a task for your tongue. With each *r* roll and each new time you say "arrivederci," your tongue becomes stronger, and the memory becomes established.

This is what I have applied to my life. I call it baby steps because of Professor Matteo and what he said. He was right about a baby learning how to walk by falling down and getting up and trying again. This is the same approach you need to take in life. There's no need to rush and to be ashamed about how you look at the beginning. You will get better. Make the mistake, and then learn from it. Don't despise the small steps in the right direction. As you continue to take your baby steps, you'll eventually be able to run.

Chapter Twelve
KEEP WATCHING

"CIAO BELLA!" WAS shouted at me so much that I assumed every girl in Florence experienced that. If I was walking alone, I heard it. If I was walking with friends, I heard it. Whenever I walked around Florence, I did my best to keep staring ahead because instructions had been given to me not to make eye contact with men. One accidental glance in a man's direction was enough of an invitation for them to start chatting with you.

As I was on my way to an art exhibit one afternoon, I made it a point to mind my own business. Out of nowhere, a man to my right said, "Ciao," and when I looked to see who it was, I heard the same voice to my left ask, "Come stai?" (How are you?)

"Bene, grazie," I replied.

I didn't skip a beat or even make eye contact. That was still enough of an invitation for this man to engage me in conversation.

"È una bella giornata, come te. Tu sei molto bella," he remarked. (It's a beautiful day, like you. You are very beautiful.)

"Grazie."

"Guarda. Il sole riflette nei tuoi occhi. Come bella tu sei," he mentioned. (Look. The sun reflects in your eyes. How beautiful you are.)

"Grazie," I said with slight irritation.

And on and on the compliments went. I kept walking because I needed to make it to an art exhibit so that I could write an article on it for the newspaper I was doing an internship for.

"Vuoi prendere un caffé con me?" he asked. (Do you want to get a coffee with me?)

At this point, I was unsure of where to go. His constant babble in my ear was distracting me. I politely declined his invitation as I stood there looking at the map on my iTouch.

He broke the silence and my concentration with, "Hai un numero perché voglio chiamarti? Ti voglio conoscere." (Do you have a number because I want to call you? I want to know you.)

"No," I said.

"Dai! Voglio conoscerti. Sei molto bella," he insisted. (Come on! I want to know you. You're very pretty.)

I was slightly entertained by his attempts and knew that our conversation wouldn't go anywhere. I allowed him to keep talking. He launched into an entire monologue about how women were like flowers and needed men to help them blossom. I kept thinking about a comment my professor had made during my opera class. She was talking about the Duke of Montua from the opera *Rigoletto*. He's a seducer.

My professor said that even though it is difficult to tell when someone is trying to seduce you, always be on your guard to keep from falling into their trap. A seducer is not after the woman, they are after the conquering of the woman. They will use sweet words and soft gestures because they know what drives women crazy. When they have you, they drop you and move on to the next victim.

"Devo andare," I said, cutting him off. (I need to go.)

"Dove vai?" (Where are you going?)

I looked at him, smiled, and said, "Buona serata." (Good evening.)

Then, I walked away without looking back.

…

After that unexpected encounter, the phrase "Any man can wear a suit" kept coming to my mind. I don't even know why I was thinking that or where it came from. To me, that phrase meant that anyone can look good. All you have to do is fix your hair, wear nice clothes, and seem nice. For a while, I had been attracted to men solely based off of how they were dressed and their physical appearance. You know where that got me? In hot water.

Anyone can make their words sound sweet enough to cover up the trap that hides underneath. Anyone can act. People are acting all the time off-screen. The only difference is that they are not winning Oscars or Emmys for their performances. God only knows what that man had in store for me that day. I'm glad that I had learned my lesson from Francesco and walked away so I could handle my business.

The fact is that we do have to keep watching. Our guards have to be up in order to protect ourselves. God has given me so much grace in my life. He knows all of the dumb decisions I've made. Dumb decisions that should have cost me my life. When I sit and think about how He spared me, I can't help but rejoice. So many times, I had felt that something was off. I'd even seen the red flags, yet I had ignored them. I had made up in my mind that because I was a good person deep down, other people were too. That was naïve of me.

I used to blindly trust strangers with my life. So many women have done that with men who say the right words and smile the right way, only to end up in a ditch somewhere. Our parents teach us not to talk to strangers as children. That lesson is meant to be applied to life forever. Trust must be earned, not freely given. If something doesn't feel or look right, don't ignore that. Pay attention to that feeling and act accordingly.

Chapter Thirteen

A LESSON FROM DANTE

NEAR THE BEGINNING of my time in Florence, I took a walking tour with Professor Matteo and seven of my classmates. He showed us the church where Dante met Beatrice and took us over to other places we were reading about. We followed him to a tiny square, which was off of the main square near the duomo, and in between some buildings. The road changed from a rough, dull grey to a smooth, polished darker grey. My professor stopped in the center of the square as we gathered around him.

"I want to show you this," he said. "If you will look closely to the ground at your feet, there will appear a portrait of Dante. It is here, close to where I stand now."

He moved out of the way so that we could look down at the pavement where he stood.

"Oh I see it; it's right there," one of my classmates said, pointing to the ground where my professor had stood.

"Yeah! There's his nose. He's wearing a hat," another classmate proclaimed.

I squinted my eyes as much as I could without completely closing them. I followed one of my classmate's fingers as it pointed at the ground. I even stood off to the side to get a different view.

"Wait, where is it? I don't see it," I said.

My professor walked over to me, put his left hand on my shoulder, and pointed to the ground at the exact spot with his right hand.

"You see?" he asked me.

"Umm... no, I still don't see it," I admitted, feeling embarrassed and ashamed that everyone was able to see it but me. All I saw was the ground. I didn't see a dip, outline, or even a change in the textures of the pavement.

It wasn't until my last months of being in Florence rolled around, where I was finally feeling comfortable and free, that I wandered back to that same spot. I was met there by some tourists who had also come to see the portrait of Dante carved into the ground. I stood in the same place my professor had told us to stand. Without squinting or straining my eyes, I was able to see the outline of Dante, with his long, crooked nose and wearing some sort of hat.

It was in that moment, when I stopped trying to force things to happen, that exactly what I needed to see revealed itself to me. The thing you need to see is already in front of you. Eventually, what you're seeking will arrive in clear sight.

Chapter Fourteen

THE END

URING MY LAST couple of months, I took a trip back to Naples with my schoolmates and ate a delicious caprese salad as my friends and I looked at Greek ruins in a town called Paestum. Hanging out in Boboli Gardens, eating the foods I hadn't eaten, drinking more cappuccinos than I had ever drank in all of my years combined, and climbing the dome and the basilica of the cathedral with Courtney also filled my last month in Florence. My professor Matteo even took me out to get tea at his favorite place, called Caffè Florian, and showed me a spot where I could see all of Florence. The view was much better than the one I got from Piazzale Michelangelo.

Weeks before leaving, I went on a hiking trip with Sean Groomis, along with eight of my schoolmates, to a town called Cennina, which was the smallest town I have ever had the liberty of staying in. I believe it only had about twenty inhabitants. We stayed in a castle owned by a man named Oswaldo, who was so old and hard of hearing, he thought I spoke with a British accent. *He* was the one with the British accent.

He had an equally old dog who fell down the stairs one night as he was trying to make it up to his bed. I witnessed it but couldn't do anything to help him out. If I had tried to help, he probably would've attacked me, like he did to one of my friends when she went to pet him. I watched as the girl who would cook us dinner every night put a rag soaked in red wine over her leg where the dog had bit her.

We hiked all day on one of the days. Our destination was a Michelin-starred restaurant that we would eat at for a late lunch before hiking back to Cennina. Upon arriving at the restaurant, we saw the owner locking the doors. He was coming back later than we could've stayed. There were no lights to guide us back through the wilderness. I was so disappointed, and not only that, I was hungry. One of my classmates had a backpack full of food and drinks. Sean Groomis had also brought food. We found a grass patch and passed around a wheel of cheese, salami, chocolate, and nuts. We ate and enjoyed each other's conversation. That time in Cennina, in the mountains away from the noise as we hiked all day and ate, was so amazing. I was truly at peace there.

I had so many times like that: times where I was with my friends, and we laughed and enjoyed each other's company. You know the times when, after you've experienced them, you feel so full and just okay? I don't know how to best describe it, but it's a feeling of being complete. It's not necessarily that they complete you, you just feel whole and fulfilled.

THE END

I spent many nights hanging out with a friend as he played his guitar and I sang. Afterwards, we strolled around town searching for secret bakeries. They weren't actually named Secret Bakery. Everyone just called them secret bakeries because not too many people knew about them, and they literally didn't have names. At about midnight, bakers started making the pastries that would fill the shops later that morning. To find the bakery, you just had to follow the scent in the air. Once we arrived at the bakery, my friend would knock on the back door. A man wearing a white smock would open the door, my friend would hand him €8 (€2 per pastry), and moments later, the baker would hand him a bag full of croissants filled with chocolate or cream.

I had eaten my fill of delicious pastries and gelato, seen some of the most beautiful landscapes and places in the world, turned a year older, learned a romance language, and had been bitten by every mosquito in Italy. My life felt so full, yet so empty at the same time. My time in Florence was meant to be a romantic getaway with God. Instead, I spent most of my time running away from Him and running after a man. It was only when I finally started devoting my time and heart to Him again—like I had done back home—that I realized that the things I ran after—mostly the men—didn't satisfy me the way God satisfied me.

...

For the majority of my life, I had searched for love. My deepest desire was to be loved by a man. I equated being chosen to being loved. Being chosen meant that I was special and worthy. The more I ran *after* love, the more it ran *away* from me. If a man that I was slightly interested in showed me attention, smothering him by writing notes, constantly texting him, telling him how wonderful he was, offering him sexual favors, and always making myself available to him were the ways that I expressed my love. I would give and give and give. The minute I took a break from giving and realized that I was getting nothing in return, I would walk away, leaving a piece of my self-worth behind.

The chasing that I did wasn't after love at all. I was chasing the "idea" of love fueled by my lust and desperation and the fear of being abandoned and alone forever. If I was with a guy who wasn't right for me, I would stick around because I didn't want to be left alone. I clearly didn't love myself. To love myself would've been to ask myself, "Is this decision going to do more harm to me than good?" Most of the time, the answer was clearly "Yes," yet I tricked myself into believing that the answer was actually "No." Loving myself would've meant giving myself honest answers to candid questions.

When I operate out of love and when I love people, I won't need to chase anyone. And if I love people, I'll be able to be honest and say, "You know, you're great; we just aren't meant to be." And I'll stop keeping them around as if they are just an object meant to fulfill my lustful desires.

Until God is enough, nothing ever will be. That was the main lesson I learned living in one of the most beautiful places in the world. Until my daily desire is to love God, I'll always go searching for love in all the wrong places. Chasing after what I thought was love didn't lead me to love, it actually led to pain. With all of that, I came to the conclusion that true love, life, and satisfaction can only be found in God. He is the true source. He is that natural spring water I so desperately thirst for. When you are walking with Him, listening to His voice, and being obedient, those beautiful moments will be even more beautiful, and they will take your breath away. He wants you to experience life and to experience all of its decadence and beauty.

The beauty of God is that He sent his son, Jesus, to be an example of what love is. He sent Him knowing that we as humans would create a lot of messy situations. Jesus died on the cross for us so that He could be the sacrifice needed to clean up our messes. Those who killed him thought they had won. Except, they didn't because He rose on the third day—just as it was prophesied. He died for every single person on this Earth. He did that so that we could witness love and know that there is someone out there who loves us.

Even when other humans in this world have hated us and have used the name of love in vain, God still loves us, and He will never stop loving us. My life now is to live for God. If He died so that I could have an abundant life, then I need to trust that He knows what He's doing and follow His lead. No more doing things my way.

Had I run to God first, all of my insecurities and the detrimental ways in which I saw myself would not have blown up in my face while living in Florence. The best thing that I can do now is to share them with you so that you don't repeat the same mistakes I made. I see people like I was: chasing pleasure only to be met with pain. And, like me, feeling confused and thinking that maybe this next time will be different, they go and do the same thing and hope that this time will create a different outcome.

It never does. It's okay to admit that you have been wrong and that you need God's help. I thought I knew it all. I turned my back on God, which was my way of saying, "I'm going to do this, even though You told me not to. I know what I'm doing." You know what He does? He says, "Okay, knock yourself out." He'll sit back and watch you fail, because you're doing what you wanted to do. He sat back and watched me fail because I was too proud to say, "Okay, God, You're right. I don't know it all. In fact, compared to You, I know nothing, so I trust You."

Why is it so hard to do that? How can I call him Lord if I don't do what He says? We may be putting our own human condition onto God, and that's where we go wrong. We may say, "This person over here betrayed me; therefore, God is going to do the same. So, to protect myself, it's best to just do what I need so that I don't get hurt." Actually, when we don't trust God, we end up hurting ourselves more. We don't need to hurt ourselves in order to learn a lesson. What I didn't see in the moment were all of the times God was showing me how much he loved me. I also failed to see all of the lessons I learned from my experiences. Florence was a part of my life and my home for ten months and will always hold a special place in my heart.

Living in Florence helped me grow, flower, and bloom. I was a seed, Florence was the soil, the experiences and the encounters with God were the sun, and the lessons were the water. Although the environment within the soil is dark, lonely, and creates pressure, it's the perfect environment for helping the seed grow. With consistent watering and sunshine, soon changes start to happen below the surface. These changes aren't visible to the people standing above and staring down at the soil. The more the seed grows into a plant, the closer new growth gets to the surface. Finally, it breaks through the top soil. The watering, cultivating, and giving the plant proper nutrients doesn't stop. In due time, the plant will flower and bloom.

EPILOGUE

Dear friend,

Thank you for taking the time to read my very first book. If you would like to talk about any of the subjects you read about in this book, please feel free to email me at kiolashei@gmail.com or call me or text me at (818) 254-9776. I can also be found on Instagram and Facebook @kiolashei.

(Please note that I am not a licensed therapist or a counselor of any kind. I am simply someone who has had experiences and has gained knowledge from those experiences. The purpose of this book was to share some wisdom with you that I have gained about life, love, and God.)

I initially didn't know what this book would look like. I wanted to write about going on adventures as I traveled around Europe. But, a book like that didn't seem to have any purpose. Someone gave me the most valuable advice about writing my book: tell stories and teach lessons. (Well, I had many stories to tell and have many more to come in future books and e-books.) I did my best to take you along on the journey with me through all of the twists and turns of living in one of the most beautiful places in the world.

I had moments of being utterly sad, broken, and depressed. I also had moments of being happy, whole, and feeling like I was on cloud nine.

I hope this book helps those who have strayed away from God, are struggling in their relationship with God, or who have experienced so much hurt that they are questioning their Christianity and if God's redemptive power is for them.

I want you to know that even though you will face obstacles, you have already been prepared to overcome them. Things will get hard, and you may feel like giving up. Please, don't give up. You have already been equipped with everything you need to conquer those battles. All you need to do is ask for His help. Say out loud, "God, I need Your help. Thank You for giving me the strength to overcome this situation, and thank You for leading me in the right direction. I ask that You dump Your love, Your power, and Your strength onto me right now." All of the power and the help are already there. You just have to tap into that power, and you have to ask for help.

After leaving Italy, I should've kept tapping into God's resources. It hurts me to admit that even after experiencing such heartbreak and knowing that running from God was a grave mistake, it took me years to finally get my act together. As you might've read in these pages, "Life is rarely so neat."

My story didn't end when I left Italy. In fact, my story got a lot worse before it got better. Although being in Italy did start my blooming process, I still had a lot of pain to address, bad habits to break, and even more healing to do.

In future books, I'll share what life was like after returning home from Italy. I'll take you on another tumultuous journey where I ran to South Korea and away from my feelings of loneliness and feeling lost about my life. In Korea, I got involved with another guy, left Korea after one year, and came back to America only to fall into the arms of a man who was the epitome of forbidden fruit. I found myself returning back to those old habits that had gotten me into trouble in the first place. In the midst of living in utter sin (again), I got my loudest wake-up call ever. That wake-up call finally pushed me over the edge after showing me how broken I truly was. That wake-up call made me start to examine my life and the choices that I had made up until that point. It pushed me to finally start my real healing process.

Patterns will continue to repeat themselves when you don't stop, heal, and learn how to do better. It took me years to finally want to learn how to do better. Yet, my journey is still just beginning.

My journey has been filled with numerous therapy sessions; filling up way too many journals; praying; crying all the time; skipping meals; surrendering my hurt to God; and feeling emotionally, physically, and mentally exhausted. Writing books is also included in my healing journey. I will continue writing books (I am even available to help you write your book) because writing is a form of healing and therapy.

My journey has also been filled with learning to take responsibility for my actions and for my life because, for so long, I just let life happen to me. I felt like I didn't have any control over the decisions I made or even over the relationships I ended up in. Well, I do have control over the choices I make. I may not be able to control the outcome, but I have the power to make choices. We all have that power.

I also had to learn about God's true character, what healthy relationships look like, and what I as a healthy person look like. I've invested a lot of time and money so that I can lead the healthy, happy life that I have always dreamt of.

Through it all, God remained faithful to me.

I want to leave you with this important message: No matter where you are or where you go, you too can experience the overwhelming, satisfying, decadent love of God. His love will fill in all of your empty spaces. His love will inhabit you, and it will show you that while there are people, experiences, and places that add to your life, He is the one who brings true satisfaction. Everything else aids in your blooming process. It is God, however, who placed you here and gave you the ability to grow, flower, and bloom.

Please don't turn your back on Him. Run to Him. Pour out your heart to Him, and invite Him into those hurting places. He's waiting for you. He wants to heal you so that you can grow, flower, and bloom into the most beautiful flower He's ever created.

Feel free to reach out if you'd like to connect.

Sincerely,
Kio

Made in the USA
Coppell, TX
08 October 2021

63703466R00095